PREPARING FOR MEDIATION

A GUIDE FOR CONSUMERS

Disclaimer

This work is not intended to be comprehensive. It is a general guide, and is not a substitute for appropriate legal advice. Neither the author not the publisher accept any responsibility for loss occasioned to any person acting or refraining from acting as a result of material contained in this publication.

Andrew Goodman has asserted his right under the Copyright, Designs and Patents Act 1988 to be identified as Author of this work.

ISBN 9781858117140

Ebook ISBN 9781858115023

Typesetting by Kerrypress Ltd

Printed in the UK

Mediation Publishing Suite 74, 17 Holywell Hill St Albans AL1 1DT, UK
www.peerpractice.co.uk

A compromise is the art of dividing a cake in such a way that everyone believes he has the biggest piece.

Ludwig Erhard

A man should never be ashamed to own he has been in the wrong, which is but saying... that he is wiser today than he was yesterday.

Alexander Pope from *Miscellanies* by Jonathan Swift

The courts should not be the places where resolution of disputes begins. They should be the places where the disputes end after alternative methods of resolving disputes have been considered and tried.

Sandra Day O'Connor,
US Supreme Court Justice

The go-between wears out a thousand sandals.

Japanese Proverb

LIST OF CONTENTS

PREFACE

After nearly three decades in the United Kingdom, the use of mediation is at last coming of age. It has been nudged into mainstream dispute resolution in family work and small claims matters, and is used regularly by more sophisticated lawyers and their commercial clients and insurers as a better way to preserve business relationships. It could be said that a civil justice system dominated by cost, severe restrictions on access to justice through the withdrawal of public funding, and a more than seven-fold increase in court fees since 2000 have each played a part in encouraging greater use of the process.

However, most disputants coming to mediation are unlikely to be familiar with the process, simply because it is confidential and does not feature in popular culture in the same way as a trial in open court. Participants may therefore be nervous and wary of what may seem to be a strange procedure, particularly the idea that it is voluntary, non-adjudicative, non-binding until its conclusion, confidential, and driven entirely by the wishes of the parties. The responsibility for finding your own solution and taking your own decisions, rather than have a judge tell you the answer, is something participants will find strange – hopefully empowering and invigorating – but still strange.

Therefore, using generic principles, and making as little reference to law and civil procedure as possible, this book is designed to provide guidance to all participants in and parties to mediation: how to engage in, prepare for and get the best out of the process.

I am very grateful to my colleagues in the mediation community that have kindly contributed to ideas for the work, especially Karena Ellis-Greenway who produced the sections on family mediation and her standard form agreement as an example, and David Daly, who kindly provided notes on workplace and employment mediation. I should also like to thank Jo Holland of Small Claims Mediation (UK) Ltd and Roger Levitt, an elite Clerksroom mediator, for kindly permitting me to reproduce their standard form mediation agreements.

There are many resources for the consumer to use. Demonstrations of family and commercial mediation can be seen on Youtube. An interactive case progress decision chart called 'Olé' can be found on the International Mediation Institute's website at www.imi-mediation.org which I recommend to those running any sizable dispute without advice.

Andrew Goodman
1 Chancery Lane
July, 2015

INTRODUCTION

This book is about mediation from the consumer's perspective. It is for those in dispute, or potential dispute, with others, who have either heard of mediation, are considering it or being guided towards it, and need to know more; or for those who have agreed to mediate and need practical guidance on dealing with the process, the mediator and the other party or parties. Lawyers or other professional representatives will find it useful, but essentially it is written for their clients and should be treated accordingly. Therefore it does not contain citations to legal process or cases except for limited references to the Civil Procedure Rules for those already caught up in litigation.

Mediation is now a prominent feature of the dispute resolution landscape. Its use is increasing in a number of areas, driven by the desire to keep disputants out of court wherever possible, and to both encourage and empower parties to a dispute to resolve problems in a way which best suits them, without necessarily reflecting the outcome that a court would determine.

For too long lawyers have been telling their clients what the law says is important. Mediation is a method of solving disputes which addresses what is important to the client, and not necessarily to the law.

As a process it enables participants to get on with their lives or business without a third party - judge, arbitrator or adjudicator - imposing a decision which certainly one, and possibly both parties, would be unhappy about, together with its potentially devastating financial consequences. Stories in the press are rife concerning neighbours who have had to sell their properties to meet the legal costs of arguing over a narrow strip of land on the boundary between them; or of catastrophic illness arising from the stress of litigation; or of general dissatisfaction with the legal process - its cost, delays, and control over the management of the dispute.

Mediation simply offers a better way. Every mediation is a learning opportunity.

Is the Court system broken?

Historically parties to a dispute have recognised that the core element in its process has been decision-making by a judge in the exercise of a function of the state: the delivery of civil justice to its citizens.

We have come to accept this as a social norm which regulates the conduct of society against an established set of behavioural principles (the law), and also as part of our cultural thinking: the trial is a focal point of many dramatic story lines in television and film, and occupies substantial amounts of newsprint. The courts are seen as bureaucratic instruments of state control, which maintain authority, reflected in the acknowledgment of enforceable rights and obligations and the need for the enforcement and execution of awards and judgments. At best they symbolize the shared values of society. At worst, the court system is broken: justice is largely inaccessible to everyone but those with deep pockets; it is time consuming; it generates great anxiety; and it is designed to create a winner and a loser. It is designed, therefore, to create a loser, which is the driver for creating great risk in the outcome, and for destroying party relationships.

Parties employ advocates or representatives who have been trained to focus on the adjudication prototype as the primary form of dispute processing. Lawyers have devised a system where it is normal for each party representative to present proofs and arguments to an impartial, authoritative third party decision-maker, the judge. He or she gives a binding decision conferring a remedy or award on the basis of a pre-existing general rule - essentially pronouncing that a party is right or wrong by the yardstick of whether or not the disputant who carries the burden of proving his assertions of fact and law to the requisite standard has succeeded.

Lawyers have therefore traditionally benefitted from a monopoly interest in representing parties in the courts - the 'right of audience'. They have developed a technical, professional jargon, which clients do not share, and created an elitist environment in which the disputant is relegated physically to the back of the court and marginalized linguistically. The parties - who own the dispute - can do nothing except abide its outcome.

By entering the litigation process they have given away control of both the management and the outcome of the dispute. To abandon that process there is generally a high exit cost - either permitting the other side to continue uncontested or at the very least pay the legal costs and disbursements of both sides.

How does mediation meet this problem?

Mediation in all its forms is a departure from this adjudicative model. It offers party control and non-lawyerly or other professional language. Because it is not confined by a formal structure, the dispute process has a wider relevance; and the decision is not based on rule-making since it is mediative (the collaborative working towards an agreed solution) and not arbitral (the choice between one only of two conflicting positions), in the sense that an agreed outcome is fundamental.

An agreed outcome - the settlement - impacts upon the parties as a therapeutic reintegration of their relationship based on compromise and the readjustment of their interests through shared gains. Basically, it is a cohesive process which draws people together: the nature of a trial or imposed decision pushes people apart. Mediation harnesses the energy generated by the dispute and transforms the process into a problem-solving exercise, rather than deciding who is 'right' and who is 'wrong'.

Unlike our court structure, informal mediation offers not only the promise of accessibility of language and form, but direct lay participation, privacy, no binding-outcome, and innovative, pragmatic, subject-specific solutions which can be far more practical than the law permits in court, because they have direct relevance to the wishes of the parties in running their lives, or their relationship, or their businesses, or their affairs in the future.

Therefore, for the present and immediate past generation of lawyers, and particularly advocates, who have been programmed that their prime function is to prove their client's case and disprove that of their opponent, the mediation process comes as an enormous jolt to their professional psyche. Lawyers create and defend legal *interests*, and *the perception of interests*, values and norms by the use of frames of reference, namely what the law says. Mediation is much more concerned with the needs of the participants - including emotional, social, relationship and behavioural needs as well as those which are financial and commercial.

Litigation takes your facts and says 'what is important to the law?' By contrast, mediation says 'what is important to you?'

Having said that, mediation is not new-age thinking. Its roots go deep into human understanding. Its use in China and the Far East go back by millennia. Even in Ptolemaic Egypt and ancient Greece mediation has been publically recorded. This puts our relatively modern legal system into historical perspective.

Nor is mediation to be derided as a limp-wristed, namby-pamby, touchy-feely, green form of justice. It has a highly sophisticated dynamic which produces surprisingly good results for both parties. It has a very high rate of success, and of participant satisfaction. And it has the advantage of producing durable settlements and repaired or enhanced relationships.

Those who understand the process, who are properly prepared, and who have an understanding of precisely what is required, can achieve real satisfaction, catharsis, and the ability to move on without rancor or bitterness. But understanding and preparation are absolutely essential to get the full benefits that are available. And that is what this book is for.

WHAT IS MEDIATION?

Mediation is a voluntary, non-binding, and private dispute resolution process in which a trained neutral person helps the parties try to reach a negotiated settlement which then becomes binding upon them, usually when reduced to writing and signed. There are many potential definitions for mediation, and there is no point in getting hung up about labels.

As a process it is entirely consensual. Although courts both here and abroad may strongly encourage, and even direct parties to mediation, no-one can be forced to agree a settlement by imposition. The mediator has no power to do so. The whole philosophy is directed at empowering disputants to make their own decisions; though in complex or commercial disputes it would be wise to accept legal or financial advice to evaluate the worth or consequences of a proposed settlement, or to compare it with the risk of going to trial. But essentially, both the process and the outcome are for the parties themselves.

WHAT IS THE LEGAL BASIS FOR MEDIATION?

Outside the court process, the legal basis for mediation is contractual. People in dispute who already have a contractual relationship may find that the contract itself specifies that resolution should be by mediation, although the courts are concerned about the clarity and detail of any such term before making it enforceable.

Whether they have an existing contract or not, parties to a mediation are required to enter into a formal mediation agreement which sets out the terms and conditions under which the process operates. Such documents have become increasingly formal and detailed, but they are important in setting out the respective rights and obligations of the parties, the mediator, and any service provider that he or she represents. Most mediators, and most provider organisations have a standard form document which will be provided on enquiry, or will be available to view online.

Examples are to be found in Appendix 2.

If the parties reach settlement they will enter another agreement, one binding as an enforceable contract. Most mediation agreements stipulate that parties will not become bound by the outcome of the mediation unless or until they have reduced to writing and signed a settlement agreement.

In many foreign jurisdictions, and under the European Directive on Cross-Border Mediation, a settlement agreement becomes binding and enforceable as if it were a judgment of the court. American mediators, working with the International Mediation Institute, are attempting to persuade the United Nations Commission on International Trade Law (UNCITRAL) that mediation settlements should become registrable and enforceable under the New York Convention on the Recognition and Enforcement of Foreign Arbitral Awards 1958.

However at present, the law of England and Wales would require a party to have to issue proceedings upon breach of the settlement agreement in order to have the courts enforce it. That position is unlikely to charge in the near future, if at all.

You should therefore be aware that the aim of the settlement is to reach an enforceable agreement (a legally-binding contract) *which replaces the dispute and its subject matter.* Hopefully neither party will need to enforce it. Statistically, performance of a mediated agreement is far higher than an obligation imposed on someone.

Within the court structure, when litigation is ongoing or contemplated, to the extent that the dispute may already be the subject of court rules concerning pre-action protocols requiring disclosure of information about a case and supporting documents, or the preservation of evidence or monies, mediation is seen as the pre-eminent form of Alternative Dispute Resolution, or 'ADR'.

> The acronym 'ADR' was introduced to underline the difference between the process of litigation in which the courts are engaged to determine the outcome of disputes, and methods of solving disputes outside the court. Paradoxically, courts at every level now favour the use of such alternative methods, including a variety of court-annexed schemes. Examples of such schemes are to be found in Small Claims Track in the County Court; Family Proceedings; Commercial Court; Technology and Construction Court; Court of Appeal (Civil Division).

ADR is to be found widely within the Civil Procedure Rules, and the use of the word 'alternative' seems incongruous. It is merely another method of dispute processing or disposal.

Other institutions use the acronym 'ADR' differently. The International Chamber of Commerce Rules define it as 'Amicable Dispute Resolution'. Many academics refer to it as 'Appropriate Dispute Resolution'. I am grateful to Grahame Aldous QC for his suggestion to view it as 'Accelerated Dispute Resolution'. For those already engaged with the court process, that describes it best.

Thus, those engaged in existing litigation will bump up against mediation at an early juncture as something proposed by the court, or the lawyers, as a method of dispute resolution, often with the threat of a costs penalty sanction if a party refuses unreasonably to mediate.

This does not mean that the legal status of the process is any different, since the parties must agree to participate, however reluctantly. If the outcome is a settlement, this will terminate the role of the court in determining the outcome of the dispute, although with the advantage of recording the agreement in the form of a Tomlin Order that will operate to enforce it without the need for new proceedings. A Tomlin Order is a stay of the court proceedings save for the enforcement of the agreed settlement (see Appendix 5). In the event the settlement breaks down, the litigation proceeds as if the mediation did not happen.

WHAT ARE THE DIFFERENT TYPES OF MEDIATION?

One of the great strengths of mediation is that the parties are free to choose a procedure that suits them. Not only is the outcome far more flexible than that offered by a court, so is the process. Such a choice, though, requires parties to have some knowledge of what is available, what they would like, and some degree of sophistication about how that choice may impact upon the resolution of their dispute.

Having promoted the idea of consumer choice and flexibility, various mediation models and their concomitant procedures have crystallised and become more formal over the years. This has been due partly to juridification - the creep of the law in dealing with such things as the role and legal liability of mediators, enforceability of clauses in mediation agreements, and principles of confidentiality and privilege attaching to the process - and also the need to train new mediators and educate parties in what to expect.

Common Forms of Mediation

The two most common models of mediation involve the parties meeting face to face with their appointed mediator in open sessions, sometimes known as plenary sessions.

The standard civil/commercial model throughout the United Kingdom and the Far East also uses separate private meetings between each party and the mediator, called 'caucuses'. In this model the mediator acts as a shuttle diplomat, conveying information, concessions and offers to the parties and meeting with them privately. This model is described in more detail later (*see ppXX*) and generally the mediation lasts for one full day or less.

The model most commonly utilised in European jurisdictions for commercial mediation, and in England and Wales for Family Mediation, keeps the parties in plenary session throughout and does not use caucusing, although the parties are permitted private time of their own. This model generally requires the parties to commit to a series of fixed appointments over the space of four to six weeks. There may also be a preliminary pre-mediation assessment of whether the parties/dispute are suitable for mediation together with an explanation of the process (in the UK Family model, the 'MIAM'; see below).

Both of these major models are in use throughout the United States, Australia and Canada.

A different analysis of various mediation models is concerned with the degree of intervention by the mediator, particularly the expression by the mediator of his or her own views of the subject matter of the dispute. While all mediators will test the reality of parties' respective stances during the course of the process, usually by asking detailed questions about their legal, technical, commercial positions, or about the viability of alternatives, most UK mediators are trained to be facilitative, that is, to attempt to bring the parties together without expressing any personal view of the merits of a particular party's argument.

Some mediators, however, are evaluative, and will provide to both sides, if required, the mediator's opinion as to that party's own merits. When selecting a mediator it is important to know whether you want or expect to receive an evaluation of your position, and to engage a mediator on that basis. That can only be done by agreement with the other party.

It is also possible to categorise mediations by the degree to which the parties come into physical contact with the mediator. Thus far, and for most of this book, I have assumed that the mediation will occur on a face-to-face basis with the mediator and other party.

Telephone Mediation

It is possible, and becoming increasingly common for parties to smaller claims to have their mediation conducted over the telephone, in a series of calls with the mediator. Small Claims Track Mediation in the county court relies heavily on telephone mediation to make it cost effective for all parties, and for the Courts Service.

Online Mediation

In addition certain private sector providers have experimented with 'virtual' or online mediation in which the parties do not meet or communicate directly. Both formats involving the physical absence of the mediator can succeed, but the task for the mediator is likely to be much harder. The European Union has introduced a Directive for the use of online mediation, or ODR, to solve consumer disputes from 2015, and this is currently being developed to run alongside the existing complaints procedures of such e-commerce giants as Amazon, E-bay and AliBaba.

The UK response to the Directive on Online Dispute Resolution for Consumer Disputes was announced by Lord Dyson, Master of the Rolls, in February 2015 following the report of the advisory group to the Civil Justice Council which was established to look at the wider potential for the use of ODR for resolving civil disputes of value less than £25,000 in England and Wales. The report is online at   https://www.judiciary.gov.uk/wp-content/uploads/2015/02/Online-Dispute-Resolution-Final-Web-Version.pdf

The group explored its limitations and drawbacks, and the issues that need flagging up to protect consumers and businesses. The principal recommendations of the report were that HM Courts & Tribunals Service (HMCTS) should establish a new, Internet-based court service, known as HM Online Court (HMOC) to provide a three-tier service, the first being an online evaluation to categorize the disputants' problem, and to offer the options and remedies available. Secondly, to provide online facilitators: communicating via the Internet, these individuals will review papers and statements and help parties through mediation and negotiation. They will be supported where necessary, by telephone conferencing facilities.

Additionally, there will be some automated negotiation, which are systems that help parties resolve their differences without the intervention of human experts. Finally, to provide Online Judges - full-time and part-time members of the Judiciary - who will decide suitable cases or parts of cases on an online basis, largely on the basis of papers submitted to them electronically as part of a structured process; again supported, where necessary, by telephone conferencing facilities.

It remains to be seen whether resources will be committed by government to meet these recommendations, involving the development of technical infrastructure and training. If so it will herald much innovation in the civil justice system.

Civil/Commercial Mediation

This process offers parties the opportunity of exploring the settlement of their disputes on a commercial or business-minded basis rather than necessarily in accordance with their strict legal rights. It is particularly valuable where, either but for the dispute, or even in spite of it, the disputants are locked in an ongoing relationship.

Where litigation or arbitration may well fracture that relationship, which is obvious in a system in which the outcome portrays one party as a winner and the other as a loser, mediation enables the parties to deal with the issues as a problem to be solved, rather than a case to be determined. It is also forward looking, with the mediator investigating how the parties can work together going forward. By contrast, the judge in litigation is generally concerned to discover what has gone on in the past, and measures his or her judgment against those findings.

Mediation is therefore better placed to preserve and enhance relationships by enabling the parties to recognise their wider interests, draw a line under what has happened, and allow the parties to move on.

At the same time it has the collateral benefits of saving legal costs, saving management time and opportunity cost, preserving the parties' reputations from what each may say against the other in court, and dealing with the entire matter on a confidential basis rather than risk our system of open justice having the argument spill over into the local, national or trade press.

The preservation of relationships is not confined to business. These may be social or sporting - between members of clubs, societies, congregations or communities, or family members, landlords and tenants, or neighbours, or work colleagues, or the parents of children at the same school.

Family Mediation

Family mediation is a way of resolving disputes after separation or divorce. In mediation, couples/individuals are helped to look at their own solutions to their disputes, more particularly since public funding for legal fees has now been degraded in this area.

Family mediation is increasingly being used to solve other types of family problems, such as

- Separation

- Parental contact

- Disputes between parent and child

- Disagreements over the care for an elderly or seriously ill relatives

- Grandparents having contact with grandchildren

- Homelessness caused by family arguments

Some service providers can offer Child Inclusive Mediation, which is offered to children involved in the relationship. This service is offered by trained mediators who work with children and is intended as a time for the child/children to openly discuss their concerns.

Since 6th April 2011, anyone wishing to make an application to the Family Court has had to consider using mediation first by attending a Mediation Information & Assessment Meeting (MIAM).

MIAMs

The Applicant/Responding Party can attend a MIAM alone, then the Other Party would be invited should the initial party wish to proceed with a mediation. In some cases, all parties attend the MIAM but are spoken to individually to discuss their personal circumstances. During this meeting, the mediator will discuss the situation of that person, and how a mediation service can assist (or other resolution service if applicable) in improving matters for that person and children/other people in that relationship as well as answering any questions there may be.

At the end of this meeting, a decision is made as to what to do next. If the Applicant wishes to proceed with mediation, a letter would be sent to the "other party". The "other party" can then attend a MIAM and decide if they would like to resolve any differences using mediation.

Mediation Sessions

Family mediation generally takes place over a maximum of five 1.5-hour sessions depending on the type of mediation required.

All Issue Mediation (AIM): covers Child, Property and finances - minimum 3 sessions to a maximum of 5.

Finance/Property or Child Only: minimum 1 session to a maximum of 3.

Professional representation in family mediation sessions is rare. The mediator will generally administer the process by setting out an agreed agenda, and writing to the parties over any intervening period reporting what had been achieved on the prior occasion/s.

Costs Involved

Depending on the service provider, a financial assessment may be made at the MIAM - Legal Aid/subsidised fees maybe available. Those who qualify for Legal Aid will receive the MIAM and mediation session free. The Legal Aid Agency produces a guidance not which may be found at https://www.gov.uk/legal-aid-family-mediation

If you are not eligible for Legal Aid, (and at the time of writing extremely few people now are) a fee will be charged for the MIAM. Should you choose to be assessed for a subsidised fee, the level of fee will vary depending on the service provider and is based on your disposable family income and the issues to be discussed - current fee levels are in the region of £85 upwards to the non- subsidised level which are in the region of £185 per session (1.5 hours).

Service Providers

There are a range of different service providers of family mediation - charitable, legal aid and private. It is important to check with service providers as to fee levels and what services are offered before committing to mediation.

With the withdrawal of Legal Aid for most family work, the Ministry of Justice is now encouraging much greater use of family mediation, which is generally done without legal representation. To that end a quality assurance mark has been awarded to professional firms of family mediation service providers, known as MQM. This should give comfort that the firm bearing it has been registered as competent to provide its services in this sector.

Workplace and Employment Mediation

As their names would suggest, these specialist types of mediation are concerned with internal disputes within the context of employment, usually involving employer/employee relationships, although not always. The basic distinction between a Workplace Mediation - we will call it "Workplace" - and an Employment Mediation - called "Employment" from here on - is that in the former tribunal proceedings have not been commenced and in the latter they have. It is not unusual, but by no means the norm, for the employer to pay the entire fee of the mediator in Employment. In Workplace again the employer not uncommonly pays the mediator's entire fee. The disadvantage with this is the impact it may have on the perception of mediator neutrality by the employee.

However the core difference is that Workplace Mediation is intended to keep the relationship of employer/employee going. Employment Mediation invariably happens after that relationship has been severed.

From the mediator's point of view, regardless of potential power perceptions, the key word in Workplace procedure is always "flexibility". The mediator can be called in to the place of employment either by the employer's human resources department or the trade unions or even (in rare cases) by an individual employee. With each mediation it is necessary to think carefully about what shape it should take. There may be cases where the paperwork tendered in advance by each of the parties is so sparse that it makes sense not merely to have advance meetings for purposes of making introductions but also to have some additional individual meetings to try and get a sense of the nature of the dispute.

The nature of the particular organisation will also be relevant: take the example of a small registered charity with a powerful yet varied management committee and an employee who feels she has been badly treated. In that sort of case, where the charity had very little money, it was appropriate to conduct two workplace mediations of 4 hours duration several weeks apart. The dispute was resolved at the end of the second three hour period by an apology being given and accepted. On this occasion the mediator followed the conventional commercial format for the first mediation and then moved from room to room, without the parties coming together, during the second.

The procedural question for the mediator is generally how long the parties should be together and how long they should be apart in their own separate rooms.

Issues are frequently similar in both Workplace and Employment mediations, for example grievances, allegations of discrimination or harassment etc. In both Employment and Workplace there is an opportunity for an aggrieved employee (or employer) to air his or her differences and, having cleared the air, this can lead to a better working relationship. But if it gets as far as a tribunal, it is probable that there will have been an irreparable breakdown in the working relationship.

As there are no tribunal proceedings in Workplace, particular thought has to be given to whether any final agreement is appropriate. An apology can be sufficient, but in some cases an agreement that an individual or group of individuals will leave, can be the only answer. The possibilities in any given case are highly flexible.

As far as the appropriate fee for the mediator is concerned. It really depends on how many meetings may be required realistically. £3000 in total for a day can be viewed as an acceptable fee, but circumstances can vary substantially between one organisation and another. The mediator may be prepared to accept a much reduced fee (e.g. £1000) where a charity is involved.

Small Claims Mediation in the County Court

In 32 county court areas, but (subject to the impact of cutbacks) eventually expanding to cover the whole of England and Wales, cases which qualify for the small claims track also qualify for out of court mediation at no additional charge. This means claims currently valued at up to £10,000 will qualify, subject to the availability of court mediators, although it is intended that eventually the value of claims will rise to an eligibility of £15,000 and possibly more. This may be the subject of change if the HMOC scheme gets off the ground after 2016.

The mediation is conducted by a trained mediator, not a lawyer or a judge, and it usually takes place by telephone. If the mediation is successful, the parties do not need to come to court for a hearing before a judge. The county court small claims mediation scheme is an important and integral part of the court service, but certain points should be borne in mind by users:

- The service is offered to all cases at the allocation stage but only some cases are selected

- Mediation is entirely voluntary and both parties must agree to take part before the mediator will become involved

- The mediator is not a judge but is trained to conduct mediations

- The parties themselves must both contact the mediator and only then will the mediator fix an appointment

- Most mediations are by telephone but can be face to face

- Mediations succeed when the parties come to settlement and avoid the need for a hearing. This saves the cost of the hearing fee which is between £170 and £335

- The process is confidential to the parties

- The judge is told nothing of what is said or what occurs during a mediation. He or she certainly does not have to express a view on the settlement.

This scheme is administered and paid for out of the Courts Service budget (although at the time of writing even this is coming under pressure). It represents a cheap option for litigants with a small value claim and is particularly attractive to consumers.

PROCEDURAL TABLE - TIMETABLE FOR SMALL CLAIMS MEDIATION IN THE COUNTY COURT

Before allocation	Parties are sent information about the small claims mediation service with the allocation questionnaire
At the allocation stage	The parties are invited to take up the mediation option or the District Judge can select the case for mediation
If mediation is selected - the case is usually put on hold for 6 weeks (sometimes a hearing date is fixed) - this contrasts with other case tracks in the County Court where a stay for ADR is usually for 4 weeks	
	Court staff notify the mediator about the case
	The parties must ask the mediator to set an appointment
	The parties are sent information about the mediation appointment and procedure and sign an agreement to mediate
The mediation takes place by telephone but sometimes in person or online (by e-mail) - the appointment is no more than an hour	
If mediation succeeds (settlement reached)	Parties sign a settlement agreement or a Tomlin order is made staying the court action permanently except giving the court power to enforce the agreement
If mediation fails	The case returns to the system for a hearing before a District Judge

The concept of encouraging out of court settlement is integral to the duty of the court to manage cases (see CPR rule 1.4 (2) (e)).

Selecting Cases for Mediation

The allocation questionnaire asks the parties to indicate if they want to take part in the mediation scheme. Parties are sent a Courts Service leaflet about mediation with the allocation questionnaire which will help you decide if you want to take this route.

Many different types of cases are suitable for mediation; for example where there is a claim for unpaid charges for any sort of service and the defendant disputes payment because they are not happy with the service provided; this includes disputes between individuals, individuals and business and disputes between businesses. The range of cases which fall into this category is vast and will include for example claims by computer experts, double glazing companies, plumbers, electricians and builders.

Non payments for the supply of goods are also suitable; the mediator may assist the parties in reaching a settlement which involves something other than money - for example replacement goods or a discount on future purchases. There is nothing to prevent the District Judge at the judge's hearings from making similar orders.

Certain types of cases usually do not lend themselves to mediation under this particular scheme. This includes claims arising out of road traffic cases where both parties are represented by solicitors through their insurance company, and neither side accepts the blame for the accident. Judges are thought to be better able to determine the amount of damages if the quantum of compensation for a personal injury claim is in dispute.

Mediation will not be suitable where there is a legal point to be determined, or if there is a disagreement about the interpretation of written documents, including the terms and conditions of a contract. At this level of claim, Government agencies, including HM Revenue and Customs and the Child Support Agency, who might consider mediation for larger sums, will be interested only in a judgment for the full amount owed, rendering mediation in these cases a waste of time.

Whatever the type of case, if both parties indicate in their allocation questionnaire that they want the case to be referred to mediation the case is likely to be suitable for mediation. Since one of the case management tasks of the District Judge is to advance ADR he or she would be unlikely to reject a request coming from both parties.

Selection by the District Judge

Even if only one or neither of the parties ticks the 'mediation box' in the allocation questionnaire, the District Judge may decide to refer the matter to mediation, and may make a direction something like this:

Sample order (stay of proceedings for settlement and mediation)

The Judge has considered your case is suitable for mediation and you are therefore encouraged to use the Small Claims Mediation Service. This service is free for court users with a current small claims case. Mediation appointments can be conducted by telephone (saving the need to come to court) or face to face; parties can also mediate without the need to speak to one another. The mediation usually lasts for one hour and is confidential.

If you would like to take this offer of mediation - or find out more about the mediation process you should contact the court mediator on [telephone number] or send an email to [email address] within 7 days of receipt of this order

Next the judge will decide whether to put the case 'on hold' for up to 6 weeks for the mediation to take place or whether to fix a final hearing date with the proviso that the hearing date will be vacated if the case is settled. The first option (putting the case on hold) results in the whole case being delayed if the mediation fails. The second option means the case will go to a final hearing whether or not the mediation is successful, subject to cancelation if settlement is achieved. These choices vary from court to court and from case to case.

In addition, the court will make provision for what to do next in the event that mediation does not take place or that mediation fails.

If the mediation route is chosen, information is sent to the parties about the mediation and the mediator receives information about the case.

What happens next

The parties receive a court order plus details of the mediation scheme in their particular area including information about how to contact the mediator. In some areas they will be asked to complete a 'small claims mediation service reply form' which they return to the mediator

It is important to note that the parties must prompt the mediation themselves. If they do not contact the mediator and ask for a hearing date it is unlikely that the mediation will take place. The key to the process is that it is voluntary and this means that the parties must volunteer themselves to the mediator and ask for an appointment. If one party still does not want to progress with mediation then there can be no mediation; courtesy alone would suggest that the party who changes their mind about mediation should let the mediator, if not the other side, know of their decision.

The parties may individually contact the mediator by phone or email to ask for clarification of the mediation process - although the leaflets provided are comprehensive and are designed to answer most frequently-asked questions.

The parties must each sign and return an 'agreement to mediate' document to the mediator before the mediation takes place.

Engaging the mediator in the process

The mediator receives the details of the case from the court - the scheme has been established on the understanding that this will be the form of the computer printout of the case from the court computer (the 'caseman' print out). This document contains a brief summary of the claim, details of the parties and the dates for filing of the court documents. In some areas the mediator will rely in addition, or instead, on the information in the 'small claims mediation service reply form'.

In the small claims mediation scheme it is not usual for the mediator to take the initiative to contact the parties. Rather, he or she will wait to hear from one or other of them. The mediator will answer queries made by phone or by email about the process. If one party confirms that they want mediation to go ahead the mediator may, time permitting, contact the other party to clarify if they wish to proceed.

The mediator will then set a time for the mediation to take place, and, if it is to be face to face, its location. The venue for mediation will be rooms made available for that purpose at a local county court, although not necessarily the court which would be the hearing venue for the hearing before the judge.

The Small Claims Mediation Appointment

- The time allowed is only 1 hour.

- The mediator has only the most basic information about the case and does not usually have any papers; information is gained gathering information and suggestions from each side verbally.

- Everything the mediator is told is confidential and the mediator will only tell the other side strictly what the other side agrees they want to be passed on.

- The mediator will emphasise to the parties that they do not take sides or decide who is right or wrong and cannot give advice. Their role is neutral.

- The format of the mediation will be shuttle diplomacy by telephone - passing messages on and hopefully narrowing the gap to achieve a settlement.

- Parties who approach mediation with an open mind will be more likely to achieve a settlement than those who do not,

- The outcome of the mediation can be something other than money - possibly an apology or an agreement to return and do the allegedly faulty work again.

- Most mediations involves the litigants themselves as litigants in person but the parties may instruct a legal representative to speak on their behalf.

The Role of the Mediator in Small Claims Cases

The mediator's Code of Conduct will be provided to the parties before the appointment (see Appendix 3). This document expresses what the mediator can and cannot do in a mediation. In addition, the parties will have received material from the Courts Service about the process.

For the appointment itself, the mediator will ensure that both parties are aware that the process is not a judicial hearing and that he or she will not take sides, or make any decision, but take a neutral role. The mediator will collect confidential information from both parties, whom he or she will speak to or meet with privately, before individually establishing what offers each party will make to settle the matter.

The parties may instruct their solicitor, a barrister or a friend to speak on their behalf. If the person doing the talking is a friend and is not legally qualified the mediator should ensure that the litigant is with the friend and approves of what is being said on his or her behalf.

The mediation appointment is time limited to one hour and therefore you should expect the mediator will ensure that parties keep their discussions within sensible time limits.

Preparation for Small Claims Mediation

The parties should ensure in advance that they are clear about what they are hoping to achieve by the court process and if they are prepared to compromise for less. They will need to be ready to set out their case clearly. Therefore it can be helpful to prepare a short 'script' of what they want to tell the mediator. Whether the script includes information they do not want disclosed to the other side this should be set out separately and they will have to show precisely what is confidential and what is not.

Where it is essential for the mediator to read key documents before the hearing these must be sent to the mediator in advance. It is helpful to calculate in advance what the cost in time and money will be if the mediation fails to settle the case and it has to go to a judge's hearing; this should be taken into account when deciding how much to settle for at mediation.

Telephone mediations

The parties may send written material to the mediator before the telephone mediation, but usually the information in the hands of the mediator is simply the written material set out in the 'caseman' print out or the 'small claims mediation service reply form' completed by the parties. The mediator will conduct the mediation by way of telephone calls individually to the parties collecting information from each party. The parties should not be asked to go 'head to head' in a three way telephone call unless they expressly agree to such a format.

Hints for a successful telephone mediation

- Prepare what you want to say - write down what you want to say to the mediator in advance

- Listen to the mediator carefully and in particular to what he or she tells you the other side is prepared to offer

- When deciding what to settle for, factor in the cost in time and money of attending a judges hearing

---

Face to face mediations

These are not the usual format of a small claims mediation. The parties plus any legal advisor or supporting friend will be invited to attend a court venue. They can expect to see the mediator individually and only to see the other party in a face to face meeting if they agree. They may be asked by the mediator to sit in the room with the other party at the start of the process so that the format of the mediation can be explained to both parties at the same time. The format of a face to face mediation makes it easier to exchange information which is set out in documents or to look at other material, for example goods that are alleged to be defective.

Online mediations

There have been successful mediations by email within the Small Claims scheme. The mediator will often be in contact with the parties by email if offers can be made in writing and communicated through the mediator this can be a helpful way to proceed. A process of mediation through a specialized mediation 'chat room' is technically possible and has been attempted but has been found to be clumsy to date.

However the EU Directive on Consumer Complaints due for implementation from 2015 requires the use of online mediation, and with developments in technology this format is likely to become a recognized feature of the small claims resolution landscape, as already discussed concerning the Government's HMOC initiative above. (See also the existing Consumer and Trade Mediation Schemes, below)

The Outcome of the Mediation

If there is a settlement

The mediator has no power to bind the parties by a judgment or decision. For the outcome to be binding it must be set out in either a binding contract signed by both parties or by a consent order of the court.

Usually, because the agreement is reached over the phone and the parties are not represented, the responsibility for drafting the settlement contract (agreement) falls to the mediator. The mediator should read out the wording of the agreement and then explain that it needs to be signed by both parties. The agreement can be sent by email, fax or by post. A sample of a settlement agreement, which follows the format often used by mediators is set out at Appendix 4 .

It is often helpful for the agreement to be set out by way of a formal order. Such orders are called 'Tomlin orders' and they need to be approved by a judge - usually a District Judge in the court where the case started. A standard draft Tomlin Order is set out at Appendix 3.

There is no court fee payable on the making of a Tomlin order in these circumstances because it is worded as a permanent adjournment ('stay') of the case.

If no settlement is reached on mediation

In the event of the mediation failing the case will go back into the system to be dealt with at a judge's hearing.

There should be no need for the parties to take active steps to promote the movement of the case to a final hearing. If the case has been put 'on hold' then the case will be automatically revived at the end of the mediation process. If the case has already been given a hearing date that date will go ahead.

Whether or not the outcome of the mediation has been successful the parties will be asked to complete a customer feedback form, for Ministry of Justice statistics.

Small Claims Mediation - Frequently Asked Questions

Can I be forced to go to mediation against my better judgment?	No - but bear in mind if you refuse to try and settle and the hearing judge considers you have behaved unreasonably you may be ordered to pay costs
I have a really good case and I don't want to settle for less than I am entitled to - must I accept less just to reach a settlement?	No - the mediation process is not meant to be a way of making parties accept less than their legal entitlement
I want to use my lawyer to represent me at the mediation appointment - is that allowed?	Yes
Is mediation cheaper than going to a small claims hearing?	A claimant who takes the mediation route saves the hearing fee, but if the case is won then the other side may be ordered to pay this expense by the judge. A mediation by telephone will be less time consuming than attending a hearing in person before the District Judge and there will be no travel and parking expenses. Claims by the Courts Service that the mediation process is free are not the full picture as the court fees paid to start the court case and the allocation fee are not refunded if the mediation is successful.

Is mediation faster than going to a judge's hearing?	It depends - a mediation will take place within 6 weeks of referral to mediation. A hearing before a judge is likely to be over 6 weeks in the future. If the case is put on hold for the mediation to take place and the mediation fails this holds up the whole process by 6 weeks
What do other litigants say about mediation?	They are overwhelmingly positive about the process. Over 90% of customers praised the professional and helpful approach of the mediators and express themselves to be happy with the outcome. They were happy with the information provided about the mediation process by the courts. For parties who do not want to go to a hearing the advantages of sorting the case out by telephone is very attractive.
What are the chances of the mediation being successful?	Of the cases which actually go to a mediation, on average over 80% result in a settlement. This figure does not include cases which are referred to mediation and where no mediation takes place. It is important to note that the parties who engage in mediation are, by definition, willing to settle
I am acting for myself and think I will at the mediation appointment. Will I be at a disadvantage if the other side is supported by a lawyer?	You might be. However, this also applies if you go to a judge's hearing. Judges and mediators alike will be sensitive to you feeling at a disadvantage.

Consumer, Trade Schemes and Online Dispute Resolution

Many consumer and trade mediation schemes are in operation. They are usually free for use by the consumer, and otherwise may be modestly priced. Many large companies are now actively involved in using technology to create interactive mediative solutions for consumer complaints. You should ask for the rules of any such scheme, either in hard copy or as a download.

E-businesses are rapidly growing in number and size and online shopping is developing at the expense of traditional marketplaces. With the worldwide recognition of the internet as a global trading platform, commerce has been the driving force behind the development of Online Dispute Resolution (ODR). Such schemes erase logistical barriers to conflict management since parties do not have to waste time and money on travel; they can solve conflicts from their offices using web portals such as Zoom. For commercial giants, such Amazon, Pay Pal and eBay, ODR represents a useful tool in reducing the cost of conflict. The rising giants of e-commerce in China, Alipay, Alibaba, Aliexpress, Madeinchina and Taobao are all developing ODR schemes as dispute resolution mechanisms that will enhance the customers' trust in online traders, be easily accessible by the final users and resemble real-life in-store complaints offered to the average, and even unsophisticated customers.

However, since ODR is a relatively new tool, questions are abundant:

- how to use ODR successfully;
- what laws and rules apply in the process;
- if a contract does not address ODR, who can take advantage of it, if anyone;
- how does one submit a dispute to ODR;
- how long does it take to reach a solution and what happens next;
- is the decision binding and how is it enforced; and,

- how confidential is it?

The law has an understandable knack of lagging behind advances in technology. However businesses need to, and should already be expected know about EU Regulation No 524/2013 dated May 21st, 2013 on Online Dispute Resolution for Consumer Disputes and the Directive 2013/11/EU dated the same day on Alternative Dispute Resolution for Consumer Disputes and the respective changes in ODR.

The new regulation provides for the creation of an online platform, an interactive website which is uniform for all member states, and which will serve as the single entry point for customers and traders willing to resolve out-of-court contractual disputes arising from online sales and the provision of service transactions. The new EU directive establishes a precise time framework for the relevant procedures, sets out the information requirements and state the quality criteria of those involved. At the time of writing there are only draft procedural rules in place, and obvious difficulties lie ahead with implementation by different member states, but consumers need to be aware that from 2015 ODR claims procedures may begin to have a significant impact on the litigation market.

BASIC PRINCIPLES

Why use mediation?

To make the decision whether or not to have a case or dispute proceed to mediation requires a wide range of information. Working through this chapter, you should aim to gain:

- An understanding of the process: what mediation actually entails, and its different forms;

- An appreciation of the possible outcomes to the dispute outside a negotiated agreement, i.e. what happens if negotiation or mediation fails;

- Sufficient knowledge of the strength of the legal case or of your current position;

- An understanding of the true value of the dispute or legal case in terms of

  (a) cost efficiency;

  (b) time efficiency;

  (c) what you really want to achieve if you can;

  (d) whether the legal remedy available from the court (even if achievable) can provide what is actually needed;

- Adequate knowledge of:

  (a) the immediate impact of the dispute on you in terms of money, time, aggravation, reputation, health and anything you may not yet have realised;

  (b) the impact of the dispute on your wider business affairs;

(c) any ongoing, or intended ongoing relationship between you and the other disputant/s - whether commercial, social, recreational or personal.

Without this information you will not be able to assess whether the decision to mediate is right for your position. It is not merely a question of applying mediation theory, or of being seduced by the ADR industry or even worrying unduly about costs sanctions in the litigation at this stage, although later this should become an important concern. You have to answer two basic questions:

1. Is my case / the dispute suitable for mediation?

2. Is the case ripe / am I ready for mediation?

IS MY CASE / DISPUTE SUITABLE FOR MEDIATION?

Very few disputes are unsuitable for mediation. Over the last few years it has become recognised that apart from circumstances where a purely legal decision is required, often to establish a principle or create a precedent, or the legal case is so strong that one party does not wish to make any concession, or the law provides relief which a mediation cannot - such as an injunction, virtually any case or dispute can be mediated.

But there can be inherent difficulties in persuading others, including partners, other decision makers or the other side and its lawyers, that this is so. For example, the benefits over cost may be marginal in the circumstances if the dispute has been in the hands of lawyers for any length of time. The mediation process may be perceived as an additional rather than an alternative procedure, and come with an additional layer of cost.

The opening offer to mediate is still regarded in some quarters, nearly always erroneously, as an indicator of weakness in a case that is being litigated. This stigma is based on the ignorance of the recipient, either of the process or the opportunity being presented, and such lack of knowledge takes time to eradicate.

In this respect the Court of Appeal and High Court now regularly threaten parties with costs sanctions if they unreasonably refuse to mediate. Such risks are present before proceedings even commence as lawyers and other professional advisers have a duty to explain mediation to clients, and the courts will do so for unrepresented parties.

The first question does, however, lead to the second question and one that is of at least equal importance.

AM I READY FOR MEDIATION?

Mediation is almost always worth trying (if the necessary parties can be persuaded), but if so, when?

All ADR processes may be utilised either before formal proceedings are issued or during the course of litigation or arbitration. Under the Civil Procedure Rules parties are required to at least attempt settlement negotiations under the Practice Direction on Pre-Action Conduct (PDPAC) which carries within it cost sanctions for a failure to meet that obligation, and the possibility of proceedings being stayed by the Court to allow parties time to negotiate or agree an ADR procedure.

To work out when to call for or agree to mediation there are a number of questions you should consider.

- Have you enough information about the claim, its defence, any cross-claim or third party entanglement?

- Do the parties know and understand the issues being raised by each other?

- Do you and each other disputant at least know his, her or its own version of the facts?

- Do you require full disclosure of documents, for example financial material, or have you sufficient to proceed?

- Do you have a proper understanding of your own needs?

- Are there non-parties to be brought in?

- Do you know how to apply pressure to your opponent by using the threat of a costs sanction should your offer of mediation be unreasonably refused? Getting the timing of the offer right may be important.

- Conversely, is the potential cost saving such that mediation should be attempted as early as possible - even before proceedings have been issued?

- Is it a dispute that will turn on expert or other technical evidence?

- Is it therefore possible to bring forward the time for mediation by obtaining early expert evidence or appointing a joint expert?

You really need to know the answer to each of these questions, not least to see if they are relevant to your situation.

Both of the key questions above should be placed in the context of meeting your best needs for resolving the dispute. As other ADR processes become more sophisticated you must consider whether mediation is a better vehicle for settlement or determination of the issues than other processes, for example early neutral assessment, which is a non-binding assessment by a lawyer or other subject matter specialist of the likely outcome of the dispute were it to proceed to some form of arbitral hearing (i.e. a trial), or a binding expert determination, or a traditional arbitration procedure. To do so you may need to learn more about these other processes.

A reference to ADR by the court does not mean considering only mediation, though many courts assume that it does. It can be as flexible as going to an advisor trusted by both sides to get an opinion ('ENE' mentioned above), and then use that as the basis for negotiation. It doesn't have to be a lawyer. It could be someone learned in the subject matter of the dispute, like a property professional. Historically it could have been a priest or an imam or a rabbi, or simply a wise elder of the community. If there is a social level to your dispute, you could find someone who is a friend to you both.

Getting Agreement to Mediate

Most lay people are extremely nervous of the court environment, and that is understandable. Going to law worries people, and so it should. It is expensive, time-consuming, rigid and inaccessible to ordinary laymen. And often the court process entirely fails to meet expectation.

But since there is an inherent respect, sometimes a sense of awe, about our judicial process, the average disputant will be even less familiar with mediation and might worry about being rushed into a strange procedure. He or she may well need convincing that a non-arbitral process will suit their need, particularly since they are likely to regard the mediator as a form of judge, which, of course, they are not. You will certainly want reassurance that your legal representatives, if any, are familiar with and can be tactically astute while using this process.

The heart of mediation

Mediators are trained to investigate the potential for joint gains in resolving disputes. *They are looking for a solution to the problem that will satisfy all sides, **not just yours**.* That is one of their most important tools in unlocking the potential for settlement. This investigation applies at every stage of the process, from persuading potential participants to agree to mediate, through to analysing and proposing constructive settlement opportunities on the day itself.

From the very outset you will have to consider whether mediation will suit both your and any other party's desired outcome. The most obvious examples are cost and time savings, certainty of outcome and control over the process. An important factor is to look at the alternatives. To persuade another party or his or her lawyers to mediate you will need to consider and identify what value there is in avoiding arguments over the merits of the case. Look outside the immediate remedies that the court can provide:

- The other party may have a strong legal case - either actual or perceived - but may be unaware of the value of wasted time; irrecoverable legal costs and expenses (known as disbursements); the time of any witnesses, employees or co-workers both in preparing for litigation and attending court; the impact of such loss of time, whether in management or production, on a business or employment; the impact of publicity; and the cost, effectiveness and time for execution of a judgment or recovery under an order.

- He or she may have a weak case, which they may not wish to test in court, or avoid an adverse precedent being set.

- There may be collateral or parallel disputes outside the strict ambit of the present case of action - further disputes that strictly fall outside legal rules (CPR Part 3.4.3) which require that the parties should bring forward all matters between them in the same action.

- There may be a further or ongoing relationship between you and your opponent, either not in dispute, or one that you cannot change. This may be commercial, social or economic, or property-related. It may extend to family relationships, that of neighbours living in close proximity, or co-employees or those with a social connection who occupy shared work or leisure facilities or social amenities, membership of clubs, the societies or even religious congregations or parents of children at the same school.

Advancing mediation as a practical solution presupposes that you are considering settlement at all. If you, or indeed the other party, are determined to have a 'day in court' at any cost, that position may well change once the true costs of present day litigation start to mount up, and to bite. Principles do not come cheap under the Civil Procedure Rules, and case management may drive you and your opponent inevitably towards mediation, whether as willing participants or not.

As to the 'day in court' argument, while a judge may provide vindication or exoneration of a position or deeply-held view, the process is hardly without risk. And, as a process, witnesses are confined to *what the law says, and not what you think* is relevant, stripping evidence of emotion and feeling, and emasculating those providing oral testimony to the mere answering of questions. Ironically, it is the mediation process that actually offers the true day in court, where disputants can say precisely what they think, what they feel, how they are affected and what they want to happen; and to do so free from interruption, protected by the process in open session, and encouraged by the mediator's empathy in confidential private meetings.

So, three important questions may arise:

First, do you, or will your opponent think that you or he are being deprived of a 'day in court' where the judge can say both to the parties and to the wider world that one of you is right? That is a matter to be dealt with in terms of litigation risk and cost/benefit analysis, and looking at what mediation can bring in terms of other gains, outside the ambit of what the court can do. Mediation may not provide vindication but it offers more significant tangible benefits, not the least of which are cost and time savings, a flexible outcome and the chance of preserving relationships. Try trading out of the dispute rather than risk economic disaster, perhaps for both sides.

Second, are you concerned that an approach to the other side to mediate may be seen as a sign of weakness? This should be dealt with by reference to what the court rules would require anyway: the Court actively promotes mediation and will punish those who refuse to consider it: practice directions concerning mediation are at CPR rules 1.3, 1.4(2)(e), 3.1(4), and the penalty costs regime CPR rule 44.5 (3). There is plenty of judicial authority to support this view.

Therefore how can it be a question of weakness to offer it to the other party?

Any initial approach could be made by the mediation service provider or by the court rather than you or your solicitor, should you have one.

Third, you will want to know how much the process of mediation will cost. Understandably your concern may be that this represents a waste of money if no settlement is achieved. Statistically mediation has a high success rate in achieving settlement of disputes, well over 50%. Some industry analysts say as much as 85%. The mediation process creates a momentum towards settlement, even if no agreement is concluded on the day. It brings collateral benefits to litigation by reducing or clarifying issues, and enables both you and your legal team to have a good look at how the other side are likely to shape up at trial.

If nothing else, mediation will inform you of things you may not have known. Certainly you are likely to hear the other party's position put in a way it may not have been previously. It could be more informal; it could be more conciliatory; it could be delivered with a completely different emphasis, or be driven by a very different agenda. The confidential nature of the process encourages parties to be more open with each other, and to worry far less about the legal niceties of their position.

KEY POINTS TO UNDERSTAND

You need to be able to make an informed choice about agreeing to mediate. At its most basic be sure you have a clear understanding of at least following points:

The role of the mediator

This process is not the imposition of a decision by a third party, but a consensual attempt to solve the problem in hand, and, where possible, any collateral or wider issues between the parties that exist or can be foreseen. You may be looking for goals to be achieved beyond the ambit of the existing dispute; or beyond what a court can do for you. Here the mediator can help, since he or she is able to do things a judge cannot. The mediator will be a confidential listener and a shuttle diplomat; will filter parties communications with each other; will absorb any emotional antagonism and push the parties to focus on underlying objectives rather than posturing or staking out a position; will encourage joint problem solving, suggest appropriate compromises, and also ask tough questions to discover and mirror to them the strengths and weaknesses of a party's case ("reality testing"); and will manage and steer the process and the parties to a mutually satisfactory outcome. What the mediator will not do is be a judge; he or she may refuse to offer non-binding views on the merits (even if pressed to do so)

Confidentiality

A legal framework exists to protect your position. In particular it operates as a safety net. The "without prejudice" and confidential nature of the proceedings mean that facts, concessions and information exchanged or obtained in the course of a mediation may not ordinarily be used elsewhere afterwards, including in the litigation.

A Consensual Process

The extent to which the process is consensual: you may leave the mediation at any point without sanction. The prejudice attaching to unreasonably refusing mediation (and therefore potentially attracting the Court's displeasure and adverse costs under CPR Part 44) should the dispute be determined in contentious litigation, does not presently extend to the Court scrutinising why you left the process. That is caught by confidentiality.

An Element of Compulsion

The mediation proposed may come under the ambit of a particular local court-annexed scheme if the dispute is contained within a certain jurisdiction. At the time of writing you cannot be compelled by the Court to mediate, but that position may well change. However even if it does, the Court has no power to compel you to accept a settlement proposed at mediation, however advisable that may be.

Settling the Dispute

Once a settlement has been agreed *and* reduced to writing and signed, it becomes enforceable as a contract. As long as it is legal, certain, workable and enforceable the courts will give effect to it, since it is governed by contract law. Just because the agreement came about as the result of a mediation does not give it any special status.

MEETING CONCERNS

The UK mediation industry has produced over the last 20 years a very large number of well qualified, easily available and fairly priced mediators, including specialist practitioners. Most mediators entirely undervalue the gift they bring to parties in dispute. Although their functions are very different, unlike a judge you can choose a mediator.

Large corporations sometimes resist agreeing to mediate, and often present a problem later in the process. In a multi-layered or institutional concern, whether in the private or public sector, the question whether to mediate has to be placed before the appropriate decision-maker by his internal advisers. In organisations where there may be a blame culture there is a risk that people would rather not make a decision, than make one and get it wrong. You may have to overcome this kind of culture and stand firm in saying mediation should be tried, and at what stage in the management of the dispute.

You may need to treat the other party with care when trying to persuade him or her that mediation will suit the situation. In many cases it is a hard decision to make not to fight a case in which he has belief, and he may be concerned reasonably about the 'blink first' mentality or what he perceives as an additional layer of costs.

These perceptions ought to be overcome by demonstrating that entry into a mediation is relatively risk-free: in a process which is non-adjudicative and non-binding you have the flexibility to act outside the constraints of court rules and to exploit the dynamics of mediation procedure to its best advantage. Even if it does not succeed, a court subsequently will give you credit for having at least tried the process. If it fails, although the costs may have been wasted, costs which are outside the scope of the mediation agreement itself will generally become costs in the court case if you proceed along that route afterwards.

Unlike the strictures of litigation, you have the opportunity to devise solutions to the problem, rather than present evidence and argument in an attempt to prove your position, and to address what the other side is saying, rather than score points from your opponent.

Can I say no to mediation?

If you seriously consider the process inappropriate to meet your needs you should know equally how to argue against being pushed into it if you have a reasonable ground to object. Most cases are now regarded as suitable for mediation, and that (short of compulsion) a judge's encouragement for parties to go to ADR may be robust and he will not necessarily accept an unwillingness at face value.

There are circumstances which will impede the court's charge towards mediation, and which may affect you. These concern situations where:

(a) At least one side requires a precedent to deal with future similar problems, and the law is presently unsettled.

(b) There is in fact (or law) no bona fide dispute - one side's position is devoid of merit.

(c) You need a legal remedy which mediation cannot achieve, namely an injunction or other mandatory or prohibitory order of the court (although mediation should be given serious consideration after a preliminary court hearing).

There are other arguments available to resist mediation, or tactical considerations by reason of which you should not engage the mediation process at this particular stage in the action. For example:

(i) The advantage of delay heavily favours one side.

(ii) The case can be settled soon through unassisted negotiations.

(iii) Conversely, there is no motivation to settle at all.

(iv) One party requires a full open court personal vindication.

(v) The case concerns criminal activity, family relationships or requires the paramountcy of the court's jurisdiction.

(vi) There are vital corporate interests involved.

(vii) Taken together with any of the previous factors, more time is needed to properly evaluate each side's position and settlement possibilities.

(viii) the opinion of an expert is needed before the decision to mediate can be taken.

(ix) There has not been sufficient disclosure.

(x) In the particular circumstances of the case there should be an exchange of witness statements first.

(xi) Where on any view the cost/benefit analysis suggests that the costs of the mediation will be disproportionate to the value of the claim.

Approach your argument against having a mediation with care and particularity. If the case proceeds to trial, even if you win, the court may well wish to consider whether ADR was unreasonably refused, and will look at all of the pertinent circumstances including the nature of the dispute, the merits of the case, whether other settlement methods had been attempted, whether the costs of ADR might have been disproportionately high, whether the delay to accommodate some form of mediation would have delayed the trial significantly, and whether ADR had a reasonable prospect of success.

Please note that your belief in the strength of the case is not of itself a ground for refusing mediation. A judge may well deprive a winning party of his costs if he concludes that mediation would have been suitable, was likely to be fruitful, and should at least have been tried. Recent law suggests that simply declining to answer the other side's request to mediate is very likely to attract a costs sanction.

How do I get the other party to mediate?

As can be seen above, despite its many advantages mediation is not a panacea, and there are cases where it is not appropriate. Timing is equally, if not more, important. Therefore you should not propose mediation to the other side unless and until you are satisfied that:

- it is appropriate for the dispute;

- you know what it is and why he should agree to it;

- you understand why it is right for you and

- the time is right.

Whatever view you take of the strength or otherwise of your own position you need to recognise that there may be serious and good faith differences between the parties' forecasts of the likely result. This operates to create a settlement gap that is difficult to bridge.

Here are some ideas which may help the other side agree to mediate:

1. If the subject matter of the dispute is contractual first see if there is an ADR/mediation clause, and, if so, whether it is mandatory and enforceable. Whether mandatory or not, the existence of the clause should be drawn to the attention of the other side at the earliest opportunity. Let your opponent have the burden of explaining to a court why it should not be utilised.

2. See if the other side's lawyers or professional advisors are members of either CEDR, ADR Group, the Civil Mediation Council, SCMA or one of the other widely recognised mediation service providers. Suggest that their opposition to mediation in your case is inconsistent with their membership of organisations promoting mediation.

3. Point out that the Civil Procedure Rules require consideration of ADR anyway. Courts are serious about using CPR rules 26.4, 1.3, 1.4(2)(e), 3.1(4), and the costs regime under rule 44.5 (3). Where appropriate invite

them to consider the practice directions provided for the specialist jurisdictions of the civil court: see, for example, Commercial Court Guide Part G

4. If the other side have no prior experience of mediation and need an independent explanation of the process, provide some educational material.

5. Show that the relevant business/social relationship might be preserved/resumed under mediation, but will almost certainly be fractured by the continuing litigation.

6. Underline that it is a non-binding process and therefore has little downside. Agreement to enter mediation does not presume a fixed outcome.

7. Where appropriate suggest that any information disclosed under the court's pre-action protocols makes it obvious that a creative commercial solution that is the most desirable outcome for the parties cannot be provided by the court.

8. Reiterate that although mediation is no longer cheap in absolute terms, it remains a cheaper option than litigation taken to trial.

9. The courts continually say that judges will consider imposing costs sanctions on parties who unreasonably decline mediation, or who ignore a request to consider it. There have been recent examples of this simply for ignoring a letter inviting mediation, which are well known, and should certainly be understood by lawyers for the other party. Courts reject the notion that because one side has a particularly strong case, or because the parties are too far apart, these are reasons not to mediate.

10. For opponents who say they genuinely do not know the advantages of mediation they are these:

    • It is desirable to be able to control the outcome of the dispute rather than have it imposed upon you, potentially leaving both parties dissatisfied by the experience. Many 'winners' find that in real terms, taking into account time, irrecoverable costs and aggravation, and the impact on a party's reputation, they have not won anything at all.

- Where each side has some merit this may be reflected in a fairer outcome than the court is able to provide.

- The absence of a trial not necessarily wanted by both parties has its advantages: reduced costs; no full trial preparation; the litigation is not so protracted; and the absence of findings of fact that might subsequently be used by one of the parties.

- Generally there is a very speedy resolution.

- Those interests which are of real importance to either or both parties will not be obscured by any technical or legal issues advanced by the lawyers within the framework of the litigation.

- There may be no real point in trying to fight against a legal principle where the determinative legal issues are already well settled.

- There may be a need to avoid an adverse precedent, and this consideration may attach itself to both sides.

- One or both parties may have good reasons to avoid the publicity which, potentially at least, is always thrown up by litigation whether at a local or even national level.

- One or both parties desires that, for commercial or other reasons, the existence of the dispute itself should not become known.

- One or both parties may have a desire to limit the disclosure they would otherwise have to provide in the course of the action.

- A party has disclosure which would be embarrassing, either in the context of the dispute, or generally.

- A party has trade or business secrets which it would prefer not to reveal but which might become public if the case went to trial.

- The case may settle before trial, and if so it is as well to try and stop it sooner rather than later. There may be no good reason why the case should not settle, but it requires the impetus of objective and outside thought.

- Perhaps neither side really wants to litigate, even though there are commercial or social pressures for doing so.

- A mediator will help diffuse the emotion or hostility that may otherwise bar any settlement.

- The uncertain outcome of a trial is generally a good reason to mediate.

If you cannot persuade your opponent to consider mediation, or if, for some good reason, you feel uncomfortable in doing so, one of the functions of a mediation service provider is to approach the other side at an early juncture to explore the desirability of mediation. So use an experienced neutral third party or a mediation service provider to break down the resistance to mediate. They will be better practised than you in dealing with the range of excuses made to evade the process because of its unsuitability for this case. They will be able to answer the typical assertions that mediation is not appropriate because the case is too complex, there are different legal opinions on the merits, the experts cannot agree, or there is too much or too little at stake.

Current judicial thought is that there is only a limited range of cases where mediation is in fact unsuitable - the desire for a public law precedent, a clear case for summary judgment, and where urgent injunctive relief is required. Even in the latter a claim can certainly proceed to mediation after an interim order is made.

The CPR and court annexed schemes mean that lawyer should no longer have a 'don't blink first' mentality, and also ironed out any stance where a party insists on pre-conditions before entering the process. The strong support shown by the court for confidentiality, affording the contents of the mediation the same status as "without prejudice" negotiations, is designed to give confidence to the parties.

Can I be forced to mediate?

The short answer is, at the time of writing, no, you cannot be forced to mediate. But you need to consider very seriously the implications of either refusing or ignoring an offer from the other side to do so, particularly if that course of action is recommended by the court or your lawyer. The consequences of an unreasonable refusal will be met by the displeasure of the court, even were you to go on and win the case. Unless you are very close to trial and substantial expenditure has already been incurred, or you need a specific court order or precedent, in nearly every case the advantages of at least trying it should outweigh the additional costs. Good mediators will help the parties find a path through the most intractable of disputes, where the impediments to settlement seemed enormous at the outset.

Even if you feel driven to mediation, or even if, in the fullness of time the court obtains the power to order it, no-one can force you to settle the case on any terms other than those acceptable to you.

Do I need a lawyer or other representative?

Again, the short answer is no. There is no right of audience in mediation (what the lawyers call *locus standi*) which obliges you to be represented by a solicitor or counsel. If you feel you need to be represented, a lawyer can attend with you, but alternatively you can so be represented by another professional, perhaps your accountant, surveyor, financial adviser, business colleague or even a friend.

Why then, use a lawyer as an advocate in mediation?

The answer lies in the skill set of the lawyer advocate, particularly one trained in mediation advocacy; the diminishing reality of empowerment; and the shadow of the law, as it impacts on party disputes.

Lawyering skills

The handicap of the lawyer's professional training and psyche is counterbalanced by his innate skills as an exponent of critical analysis, of problem solving and of communication in circumstances where dynamic change is part of the dispute process and has to be reacted to and catered for. The lawyer is trained at absorbing and processing information to provide insight and better understanding of the conflict dynamics, of finding new ways of reaching agreement by clarifying the perception of issues, sharpening the parties understanding of interests, and identifying the means of viewing the subject matter differently, or at least identifying those differences which cannot be bridged and which may have to be set aside.

That is a fancy way of saying that people who buy legal services have a problem they think needs a legal fix. Sometimes it does; but sometimes it doesn't, and they can do it themselves. Much depends on what would happen if mediation did not bring about settlement. If the dispute went on to litigation, or an existing claim went on to trial, it is probably better to engage a lawyer, particularly one who was trained in mediation advocacy, for example a member of the Standing Conference of Mediation Advocates (www.mediationadvocates.org.uk).

The benefit of using a lawyer who has been trained in mediation strategy, dealing with the mediator and negotiation techniques, is to secure a better settlement than would otherwise have been achieved without him or her. You will have to weigh up whether it is cost effective to do so, but if you are already engaged in litigation, your lawyer is best placed to tell you during the mediation what will happen in the event you cannot get a satisfactory settlement.

The reality of empowerment

One of the central arguments put forward by the proponents of mediation is that it operates as a means of settling conflict that leaves responsibility for outcomes in the hands of the parties themselves, rather than have a decision imposed by a judge or reached by bargaining between partisan lawyers. The parties decide what suits them, and for sophisticated parties this can include the process and its management.

However the idea of 'client empowerment' is undermined to some extent both by the activities of the more evaluative mediator and the development of a more formal structure by private sector mediation service providers, and state-sponsorship in court-annexed schemes.

This has given rise to a creeping juridification of those forms of mediation which operate within the fringes of the mainstream civil jurisdiction in England and Wales: a body of law is taking hold of mediation in areas which concern

- Validity of the mediation agreement

- Confidentiality of the process

- The existence or otherwise of a 'mediation privilege'

- The enforceability of settlements obtained in mediation

- Mediation under actual or implicit duress by the courts

If you are caught up in litigation the court may want to intrude into these areas, and your interests are best protected by a lawyer who can deal with such matters.

The shadow of the law and court-annexed procedure

Court agendas include large portions of routine administration and supervised bargaining. For example in divorce bargaining involves maintenance, child support, residency and care of children, and the division of matrimonial property, and often one class is used to offset another. This concept of bargaining is both widespread and can be seen in many complementary transactional or social relationships (husband/wife landlord/

tenant purchaser/supplier) where each is based on the mutual dependence of activity.

Such bargaining counters exist within the court structure and its process - delay, cost, the uncertainty of outcome, imponderable factors such as the adequacy of proofs, the exercise of the Court's discretion, the preparation of the lawyers, negotiating skills, an ability to respond to deadlines and emergencies, and an ability to recover or bear costs.

As courts have become more remote, more professional and, in England and Wales after 1999, much more expensive, they are less places for individuals to air and resolve everyday disputes and more the province of professionals and a place for the extension of government concern into areas of life previously unregulated by the state, e.g. environmental, health, safety, welfare and institutions dealing with state-dependent clients.

To an extent there has been a perceived separation of the law from ordinary citizens in terms of cost, complexity, delay, and the jaundiced view has gained ground that there was too much law and not enough justice. In England and Wales this was given credence by, among other things, the approach of Lord Denning as Master of the Rolls. This notion was, and remains fed, by the enormous growth of regulation by the state in most spheres of everyday existence, and the continuing media-driven myth of the litigious society: "blame/compensation culture" masks the significant trend that access to justice in the courts is in severe decline.

The process of the "day in court" has been redeemed by bargaining and shut-off points due to a huge shift in politico-judicial philosophy, - namely that settlement is good, judgment bad, is driven by intensive case management and supported by changes in institutional practice including the withdrawal of state funding, the embrace of ADR and the outsourcing of dispute processing to other institutions.

However, and to the detriment of the development of a culture of mediation, the trial holds a pivotal place in popular culture, with very little public or literary consciousness of mediation activity. What this means, for our purposes, is that at the outset of a conflict the disputant will normally seek the assistance and comfort of his lawyer as a hired gun, or champion, before the actual dispute procedure has been identified. Popular culture is not yet sufficiently sophisticated to recognise that mediation is not, or not necessarily, a legal process akin to a trial, and the mediation industry has done little to increase public awareness of the distinction in an attempt to create its own mystique.

The Changing Role of the Lawyer

At its heart mediation is a form of intervention in which the lawyer - or more particularly the litigator or dispute resolution specialist - acts as gatekeeper of the dispute. He or she will practice roles which are not the same as that in litigation, where primarily the lawyer is regarded as the articulate and knowledgeable party representative.

Mediation allows for the role of the lawyer to take on interventions of much more subtle variation and degree: informer, adviser, interpreter, advocate, ally, surrogate, manager, evaluator, facilitator, friendly peacemaker, repressive peacemaker, negotiator and healer. There may well be more. During the various stages of the mediation a lawyer trained to deal in the process may play any or all of the roles as part of his retainer as mediation advocate.

Lawyer or Non-Lawyer Advocate?

All litigators must now have a basic understanding of mediation principles to be able to act in an advisory role. They not only have a responsibility to identify cases, both pre-and mid-proceedings, for which mediation is appropriate, and to explain the mediation process to clients and other legal professionals. They have specific tasks within the process, and if retained can be expected to help with the following -

1. Deciding to and persuading others to engage in the process

2. Choosing the mediator

3. Controlling the pre-mediation element

4. Team leading at the mediation

5. Securing a working settlement

As advocates, they must be able to deal with all aspects of mediation within case management, something probably outside the remit or capability of non-lawyer mediation advocates. One such example concerns the enforceability of contractual mediation clauses. Most court schemes implicitly recognise a fairly formal facilitative model with a structured process, and consequently lawyer advocates will invariably use this model.

However, the courts do not necessarily regard mediation as a species of new procedure. This suggests that there are some aspects of working in mediation advocacy which will remain the preserve of the lawyers, particularly where the case starts in litigation and moves into mediation only after commencement of proceedings or when imminent proceedings are contemplated.

What are the costs involved?

The appointment or intervention of lawyers in the mediation process adds considerably to its cost. As a process mediation is still relatively inexpensive in itself, but the use of lawyers can really inflate the overall position.

Most lawyers will charge the same hourly rate for working on a mediation as they do for any other contentious business, and should you require a barrister, you can expect to have to pay a similar amount for a day as would be the cost of a trial. You need to make sure that the presence of lawyers adds value to the process and is cost effective for you. Don't be afraid to ask your lawyer exactly how he or she sees their role on the day. For family mediation it is unusual and discouraged to have lawyers present.

The plethora of available mediators in the market means that by comparison, mediators are priced very reasonably. A mediator may well be charging less than any of the lawyers in the room. He or she will expect the fee to be split between the parties, and paid in advance. There may be an additional room hire cost.

Payment to the lawyers is a matter between lawyer and client, and, if the dispute does not settle and has to proceed to trial, such costs may be claimed in the court proceedings if ongoing.

How do I choose my lawyer or representative?

The choice of a lawyer is very personal and factors will include cost, expertise, reputation, efficiency, success rate, and client concern among others. Both the SCMA (www.mediationadvocactes. org.uk) and the IMI (www.IMImediation.org) maintain lists of specialist practitioners who represent clients at mediation.

You may find it useful to ask your intended lawyer or mediation advocate a number of questions before hiring that person. I am grateful for the observations here of Beverley Tarr, a distinguished Chicago-based divorce mediator, given at the 6th World Mediation Organisation Symposium, Berlin, June 2015.

Have a candid discussion with at least two potential advocates first and find out:

- Do they trust the process?
- Are they creative?
- Will they guide you in a positive manner?
- Are they senior enough within their firm (not to be influenced by the conflicting needs of the practice to make money out of your dispute)?
- Do they have a genuine desire to help you solve the problem but not at all costs?
- Are they good negotiators?
- Do they have interpersonal skills?
- Are they adaptable?

EARLY PROCEDURE

How do I choose a mediator?

You may be engaged in a process by which a mediator is appointed, for example using the small claims mediation service, or a selection of names is given to you by a mediation service provider, but for most civil, commercial, family, workplace, employment and community mediations you will be given the opportunity to choose the mediator. If you are represented, that is one of the important tasks of your professional adviser. If he or she is experienced in a particular field or has represented parties in successful mediations before, he will have a list of appropriate individual mediators or be familiar with a service provider that operates an approved panel.

For a disputant, or indeed an advocate, the ability to choose the composition of your tribunal is an unusual and illuminating experience. Although it cannot be stressed too highly that a mediator has no arbitral powers and is not going to be a decision maker, you and your opponent will undoubtedly respect him or her as a figure of authority as the chairman and convenor of the proceedings, and will rely upon his gravitas, professional qualification and experience as a mediator. He will in fact assist in adjudicating on procedural matters, usually by providing direction and making positive suggestions with which you may be expected to agree. Invariably you may regard him as a sort of judge, even though you must understand he is not.

When available, the opportunity to select the appropriate mediator should never be wasted. Guidance over the selection is no less a function of the advocate than any other pre-hearing advisory work, and should be approached with care. If you ask your representative to advise you at an early stage in the dispute there are two important practical questions to consider in choosing a mediator. First, should a mediation service provider be appointed? Second, should the mediator himself or herself be a lawyer, do you require an expert in the area of the dispute, or else an experienced layman (i.e. non-lawyer).

You are looking for a mediator who has a number of qualities. Apart from having obtained an appropriate qualification from, and continuing professional education or current accreditation with, a recognised mediation training body, you need a person of reasonable experience having some knowledge of, if not expertise in, the area of the dispute. He or she needs to have a good bedside manner, with the common touch - hand holding is an integral part of the mediator's skill, since he also requires patience, and the ability to absorb your or your opposing party's frustration, anger or anxiety. You will want as a candidate someone with innovative ideas or problem-solving skills who is a good communicator, and exudes a sense of authority without pomposity. He will himself need to be an advocate in the sense of being proficient in examining and testing both parties' stated position and to deal readily with the consequences.

Who is the right mediator for me?

Whether you opt for a mediation service provider or not, you still have to decide or agree who is the right mediator for you. Presupposing that those institutions who train mediators provide accreditation and continuing education to a set quality threshold (maybe that prescribed by the Civil Mediation Council or the Family Mediation Council), and that the procedures, method and practice in which each train their own particular mediators are broadly similar, the question for you is how to match the most appropriate and desirable mediator to your dispute. Ultimately it may be the pragmatic questions of cost or distance or availability, but there are preliminary questions.

First, consider whether you want a mediator who is also a lawyer by professional background, if not actually in practice. The advantages are readily apparent: experienced litigators and counsel develop well-honed practical skills in critical analysis, problem solving and communication. They can be incisive in identifying key issues and focusing upon the factual and legal merits of a particular position. A mediator who is familiar with the area of law in question can, if called upon to do so, engage in debate on the law, know the key cases and recognise the legal merits of the parties' respective positions. A lawyer may also have practical experience of litigating disputes of the type being mediated.

> Specialist lawyer mediators will readily understand the legal and commercial context in which the dispute sits; they will gain the respect of both advocates and their lay clients more quickly; there need be no time wasted in laboured explanation; should you be concerned over their role in the context of your dispute, the lay parties' suspicion, wariness or frustration may thus be minimised. They will be aware of procedural timetabling, case management and the impact of costs in the litigation.

Having said that, a non-lawyer mediator may have a completely different overview of your settlement objectives as a party. He is far less likely to be concerned about legal practicalities or niceties, and will be less interested in whether or not you will be able to prove your case to a court on another occasion. In that sense a non-lawyer mediator may be of greater appeal to a party that has an obviously weaker case in law, or is far more interested in a business-orientated solution.

You should be aware that a non-lawyer mediator will not welcome being tied down to arguments concerning the legal aspects of the dispute. He or she may make you feel undue haste in getting to the horse-trading part of the process. He may be keener than a lawyer mediator to get to the heart of the problem and separate it from the legal parameters. In that sense he will not be terribly concerned about your legal interests, since his objective is to find a solution to the dispute using means that may well fall substantially outside the legal constraints and procedures that you associate with the litigation. If such a mediator makes you feel uncomfortable please remember he is not a judge, and neither his task nor the process itself is intended to impose a settlement on you. You still bear the ultimate decision of acceptance or rejection.

Both your representative, if any, and lawyer mediators need to guard against a strictly legal analysis of the dispute. This may be difficult for all lawyers. The importance of analysing a dispute in the broadest terms and not confining it to its strictly legal nature is underlined by the approach of mediation training organisations when teaching new mediators to distinguish between facilitative and evaluative mediation. Evaluative mediation is essentially opinion forming, and lawyer mediators have great difficulty in refraining from making value judgments about the parties' positions. At least they can learn to restrain themselves from expressing an opinion unless expressly called upon to do so.

With a plethora of mediators now available the expertise and experience of your potential candidate is of real importance. You have the ability to select for your mediation a mediator who is an acknowledged authority in his specialist field, be it medical, technical, financial or legal. He will be able to identify most known solutions to common problems in that area and, hopefully, adapt them to fit your and your opponent's particular circumstances.

In certain circumstances you may consider that a non-lawyer, non-specialist mediator happens to be the right person, particularly if he comes by recommendation to you or your party. You need to feel confident that he will observe confidentiality; that he will exercise control over the proceedings, and certainly that he is able to control time; that he will keep all parties informed of what is going on; that he is patently neutral, and remains so throughout the process; that he has sufficient gravitas and authority - a particular advantage of those rare occasions when using a former judge might be a good idea; that he has no personal agenda, is not a bully, will be even-handed, patient and an innovative problem solver, whether evaluative or facilitative. The European Code of Conduct for Mediators has specific provisions about impartiality and confidentiality – see Appendix 5.

You may be offered co-mediators if there are a large number of parties or issues. Under such circumstances a single mediator may not be able to have sufficient creativity, or indeed time:

mediator teams are useful in working with parties to build up trust and dealing with cultural or jurisdictional differences. A mediation team can be mixed between a lawyer and an expert, or mediators from or experienced in the separate cultures or jurisdictions. The appointment of a mediation team means that more than one activity can take place simultaneously at the appointment. Where a mediation team is involved, one solution that is sometimes adopted is to re-constitute as a form of arbitral hearing involving findings by a member of the mediation team who has not previously engaged in any confidential discussions. Whether or not a mediation team adopts such a solution, it is crucial that the members have complementary skills and work well together.

> In the article *'Choose Carefully: All Mediators Are Not Created Equal'* from his series *Mediation Strategies* the well-known Californian mediator, Lee Jay Berman, advises if a mediation is going to have a chance at success, perhaps the most important decision is who will sit in the neutral chair at the head of the table. From case to case, that decision will vary. You must invest the time in investigating, strategising and selecting the right mediator for each case. For full text see www.mediate. com archive material and the SCMA website newsletter archive at www.mediationadvocates.org.uk

Berman suggests that in a time when we have retired judges, litigators, transactional advocates, and professional mediators available, and when more mediators are specialising in particular areas of practice, the best way to select the right mediator requires a strategy.

He recommends, among others, the following considerations

- Do not select on a least objectionable or lowest-common-denominator basis. Mediation has a greater chance of settling the case if all parties believe in the mediator's reputation, personality and qualifications.

- Just because the other side has proposed a mediator that they have worked with before, that is no reason to object to that mediator. The mediator has no ability to make you agree to anything you don't want to, nor can he or she coerce or pressure you. If the other advocate is proposing a mediator they are probably doing so because they feel that mediator at least can be trusted and has a client rapport, or has the ability to settle the case, which means finding mutually agreeable terms for settlement.

- Consider the level of actual mediation training your mediator has. After all, if settling the case was easy to do, you wouldn't need a third party to assist you and your opposite.

- Consider the mediator's record for tenacity to see the case through to resolution. A mediator can only keep going if they have the skills to keep trying different things, and if they have what some have called "an iron rear end" and are willing to sit and keep working for as long as it takes to get a case resolved. That tenacity, or resolve to settle a case, is one of the most important features to look for in evaluating a mediator, and in seeking recommendations from others who have worked with that mediator in the past.

- Ask the other side, or their lawyer, about the type of mediator to which they would best respond. Some cases (and sometimes your opposite number) require an authoritative voice of a retired judge or litigator with decades of experience. Others may respond better to a persuasive, personable mediator who reaches people well and can see the big picture. Some cases require a macho authority figure, while others may do better with a more sensitive touch. It is important to consider variables such as these in each case.

- Consider whether you want your mediator to provide more of a facilitated negotiation or an evaluative appraisal of the case.

- Think about what's important to you. If you or your opponent are strongly motivated to the point of being emotionally driven by the argument, you will benefit from a mediator who can handle emotional parties and help move them to a place where they can make a decision, gently guiding the case to a smooth settlement. If parties are stubborn and intransigent, they may need logic and tenacious persuading. If they are weak decision-makers or are unsure about the fair value of their case, they may need the authority of a retired judge or seasoned litigator.

- Consider your own strengths and weaknesses. You have to be honest about hearing criticism of yourself. This may be the hardest part, but it is critical to know yourself with clarity. For example, if you have a strong, authoritative presence, you may benefit from a mediator who has a softer touch to complement you. If you tend to be more left-brained, or a more logical or linear thinker, you may want a mediator who is more right-brained, more emotionally attuned, and perhaps creative.

- Consider the timing of the case. If your case is directed towards mediation by a date that you believe is too early in the case, and you are unable to persuade the judge of this, then you will want to select a tenacious mediator who is dedicated to following the case through the litigation process. Experienced mediators know that sometimes, the early mediation appointment is only the start of the mediation process, and that additional key disclosure may be required before a final settlement can be reached. You will want a mediator who is a real believer in peaceful resolutions and in not letting litigation get out of control unnecessarily. This could range from a no-nonsense retired judge to a former general counsel to a non-advocate mediator with business and economic sense.

- Consider the subject matter. It is not imperative, but it is helpful to have a mediator who understands the nature of the dispute. If the dispute is dissolution of a family business, it can be helpful to have a mediator who understands partnership, business and contract law. It could also be beneficial to have a mediator who is familiar with the workings of the particular industry in which the family operates their business. It may be even more beneficial to have a mediator who specialises in, or understands the unique dynamics of family businesses. The important thing to consider in selecting the mediator is that they are familiar with what it takes to discuss the issues and to reach a resolution. It is not enough for the mediator to understand the legal issues; he or she must understand how to relate enough to the parties and their legal team to bring the parties to a mutually agreeable resolution.

- Consider the level of difficulty of the case. Many smaller cases can be less complex, such as a simple debt collection or personal injury case that most mediators might be able to resolve. Other cases are the type that only a small percentage of mediators can settle. For example, a wrongful death case may include legal issues, insurance coverage issues, medical issues, deep emotional loss issues, and structured settlement issues, and will require a very experienced mediator with lots of tools and skills. You will benefit by trying to match the skill level of the mediator to the difficulty level of the case. Remember, some advocates will look at a very difficult case and assume that any mediation will fail, so they will pay little attention to the selection of mediator. Instead, try hiring a highly skilled mediator and give the mediation process a real chance to get the case settled.

- Ask anyone you know who has been involved in a mediation for useful information as outlined above. Ask specific questions about each of these points, rather than simply asking if your colleague/friend/aunt liked the mediator or thought he or she was competent. Even less informative is asking whether the case settled, since there are so many variables involved in whether a case settles or not, this may be the worst indicator of the mediator's skill and effectiveness.

As Berman says, the selection of your mediator may be the most important decision you make regarding the mediation. Take the time to read through CVs, ask colleagues, and do the appropriate research, taking responsibility for making it succeed. After all, there are few experiences more frustrating than putting several hours of hard work into a mediation, only to have it fail. Make the decision wisely.

Mediation Service Providers

The great advantage of using a mediation service provider is the provision of administrative support, and a package which, for a global fee paid equally by both parties, will usually consist of:

- the supply of a recommended mediator on an approved list or accredited panel,

- his or her preparation and attendance,

- locating and hiring as necessary the venue,

- the management of the process from agreement to mediate until its conclusion.

Management of the process normally includes:

(i) providing explanatory material on the process itself;

(ii) identifying a shortlist of approved or accredited mediators experienced in such disputes, together with c.v. or résumé for each;

(iii) supplying an up to date standard form mediation agreement into which the parties will enter, together with the mediator;

(iv) agreeing and settling the mediator's instructions and remuneration;

(v) booking and dealing with the owners of the venue;

(vi) meeting any queries or problems raised by the parties, or the mediator;

(vii) co-ordinating the arrangements with the parties' lawyers;

(viii) conducting any post-mediation procedures.

There are now dozens of mediation service providers, ranging from training organisations, academic or professional institutions and trade bodies to private commercial firms. Absent using such a service most experienced mediators can be contacted directly, and this is even more so in the field of family mediation where registered providers advertise widely on the internet. For community mediation, local authorities and charities tend to act as mediation service providers.

You should choose a service provider with a substantial panel of mediators whose recommendations you can trust. You are looking for an organisation that will identify the right mediator for your dispute, and not merely nominate the same few, albeit highly experienced mediators, irrespective of the subject matter of the dispute, who are their trainers or faculty members. Its panel should have broad areas of expertise, and it must provide a fully administered service. This avoids contact directly with the mediator over minor but important details, which is potentially likely to increase costs, although the whole point is to obtain a packaged service for one fee.

A fully administered service will:

- Help the parties agree the appropriate resolution process to use;

- Encourage reluctant parties to engage in the process;

- Advise on the appropriate mediator or neutral, or, where necessary and appropriate, the team of neutrals;

- Undertake and obtain a conflict check from the neutral;

- Provide as necessary a declaration of the neutral's independence;

- Negotiate the neutral's fee on behalf of parties and deal with his or her remuneration;

- Advise on the contents of the documents bundle;

- Advise on the contents of the case summaries;

- Seek to achieve balance between the parties attending the hearing;

- Secure from each party an agreement to the terms of the mediation or provide a standard form agreement for adoption, or as the basis for further discussion and amendment to suit the particular dispute;

- Secure and organise the venue, dealing with any problems that may arise;

- Provide the mediator with engrossed copies of the mediation agreement for signature by the parties on the day of the hearing;

- Deliver the appropriate papers to the mediator;

- Generally ensure that the process goes smoothly.

When selecting a service provider you should check precisely what the fee will include, and that the service provides all of the preceding matters. Fees may be negotiable.

What is the mediation agreement?

The mediation process is entirely consensual and needs to be formulated by agreement between all of the parties and the mediator. Since it is a confidential process all attendees may need formally to be bound to the confidentiality provisions.

Despite the fact that mediation service providers, or indeed mediators working independently, will provide each of the parties with a current standard form mediation agreement which they have devised, a lawyer should review and, if necessary, revise the mediation documentation with input from the client. It may well be that someone with far more mediation experience than you has settled the agreement, but those appearing in mediation must take their clients through the document so that its terms are both comprehensive to the dispute and fully understood.

If you do not have a lawyer representing you there are certain key points which must be found in every mediation agreement, and which you need to understand:

(i) The entire proceedings are confidential and without prejudice.

(ii) No party may call the mediator to give evidence in later proceedings of what he has learned in the course of the mediation. This prohibition extends to the mediator, and the mediator's right of confidentiality will extend beyond the pre-existing dispute to cover the entirety. This prohibition extends to costs proceedings.

(iii) The process is voluntary: any party can call a halt to the proceedings without sanction.

(iv) The mediator's role is to facilitate a settlement, not to pass any judgment or make any findings.

(v) The terms of any agreed settlement are to be in writing.

In addition to these fundamental provisions, it is possible to agree the format or contents of the mediation by the insertion of agreed protocols into the agreement.

Examples of such usual clauses as these are:

- The parties will have authority to settle on the day.

- The parties will observe the mediator's directions.

- The parties will remain at the mediation for a minimum of one private session each.

- The mediation may be terminated in the event of a specified circumstance.

- The parties will not record/tape the mediation sessions.

Some standard form mediation agreements now extend to fairly sizeable documents with explanatory notes and guidance as to the conduct of the mediator. Good examples of some of these are to be found at Appendix 2.

Where institutions, such as the Royal Institution of Chartered Surveyors, acts as the mediation service provider, the standard form agreement attaches to that body. Certain terms and conditions in mediation agreements may be reflective of the requirements of the mediator's professional body (e.g. the Law Society or the Bar Council) or of his or her standards authority or professional indemnity insurers.

How do I choose a venue?

Unlike litigation, which is administered at fixed court sites depending upon their jurisdiction, you will have the opportunity to consider the most appropriate location for the mediation appointment, and should do so in terms of geographical convenience, cost of hire, nature and extent of the rooms available, but also in terms of strategy.

First discover whether the cost of the venue is included in any global fee. This should be the case if a mediation service provider is being used, otherwise there may be a separate hire charge raised. If an additional cost is being incurred consider whether it may be preferable to have the mediation cost free at the offices or chambers of one of the parties or their legal team. Identify from where your attendees are travelling, and where the other side and the mediator are located, and propose the most central location where facilities are available. Mediators consider that reaching agreement on matters such as the venue and format of the mediation session is an important psychological step towards settlement; at least it moves the parties from areas of disagreement towards areas of agreement prior to the meeting.

In a two-party mediation a minimum of three rooms are usually required, one large enough for all participants, and two for private sessions, but in family mediation one will do. For civil/commercial mediations, where there are only two meeting rooms, one party will have private sessions in the plenary room. If there are insufficient rooms for the numbers attending, parties may have to make do with corridors, which is unsatisfactory. If the availability of rooms is generous the mediator may take the opportunity of having small parallel or simultaneous meetings between, for example, the experts, or the lawyers, while he pursues settlement avenues elsewhere.

Whoever or whatever organisation hosts the mediation session, refreshments will have to be provided during the day and made available should the session go into the evening. The rooms should be accessible, comfortable, lit with natural light and heated, since parties may be occupying them for lengthy periods. The parties' rooms need to have outside telephone lines, and the host should make available wi-fi or broadband, fax and photocopying facilities, the first three to obtain additional information or documents, and the last to ensure that any agreement is copied and distributed to all parties and the mediator prior to leaving the building, and afterwards to the mediation service provider. If at all possible, the venue needs to be staffed into the night, and information should be made available to the parties concerning local transport including taxis, last train times, parking availability after business hours, and local restaurants or takeaway services.

Strategic and tactical considerations often revolve around the question should the mediation take place at your side's, their side's or a neutral venue? Occasionally parties to a dispute, particularly defendant's solicitors or insurers believe that there is a tactical advantage in having control of the venue and requiring the claimant to attend their premises. If this is seen as a form of intimidation it will hardly be conducive to settlement. If having the mediation at one party's premises is genuinely, or can be portrayed as, a convenient cost-saving device, that is more acceptable. Invariably the mediator will prefer the parties to meet at a neutral location. For you the most important thing is that you should feel comfortable and believe that the location, as in all other things, is a demonstration of the even-handedness of the process. You should not be put under pressure to accept a situation you does not want, nor feel you are being inconvenienced either by the other side or the mediator.

How do I fix the mediation date?

Once the decision to mediate has been taken and a mediator has been appointed the date for the mediation should be fixed as soon as reasonably possible. The mediator will generally be chosen according to his or her diary commitments with a view to mediating within a relatively short time period. Since key benefits to the parties are the intended savings in costs and time when compared to running the dispute in litigation, you need to take advantage of the momentum of the parties having agreed to mediate and having agreed the particular mediator's appointment. If litigation is running it is important to suspend the running of time in the action and to stop the costs clock by halting any wider investigatory, disclosure or other procedural work. In the meantime you can run the mediation as a limited, self-contained entity for the purpose of costs.

While there is certainly a strong element of pre-appointment preparation to be dealt with, and occasionally pre-appointment meetings or dealings with the mediator, generally you should aim at a delay of no longer than three to four weeks between the appointment of the mediator and the mediation itself. Often a factor in agreeing the mediator, or his services being procured by a mediation services provider, is his availability. Arguably getting an early date for the mediation is more important than worrying about preparation time. If you are aware that extensive preparation will be required, or the attendance of key personnel, or experts, that is a different matter and the appointment will have to be delayed. But once the decision to mediate has been made, the process should be driven forward and not allowed to lapse by inactivity.

Sometimes it is difficult to get everyone to agree a fairly early date, particularly since a minimum of three people's diaries are involved, and potentially many more. Build upon the convenience of the mediator, parties, essential attendees and others, in that order. Worry less about the availability of lawyers.

PREPARATION

What documents will I need?

It may be a broad generalisation but documents rarely play an important part in mediation, and the production of bundles comparable to a trial is certainly unnecessary on most occasions. That is because you are not trying to prove your case, although it may be vital to your negotiating stance that the mediator and the other side are made aware of how you see the strength of your position, which presumably, you will be able to support with objective documentary evidence. The strength of the legal case is ever-present as a frame of reference, but bundles should be minimal, perhaps the equivalent of a jointly agreed core bundle comprising only key documents and, if the dispute is in litigation, the salient court documents. Even for a moderately sized claim, the mediator will probably not want to see more than 100 pages of documents.

Of course the mediator will need sufficient material to 'hit the ground running' since he or she is being asked to guide the parties in only a few hours to the resolution of a dispute which is likely to have been running for months if not years. He will need such time as you consider necessary to absorb the facts and key arguments, undertake some background research and consider possible strategies in advance of commencing the negotiation.

The typical fee for the mediator will only allow for a relatively short period of preparation, unless additional reading time is specifically agreed beforehand. Bear in mind what the role of the mediator is going to be. There is no point in running up a bill for lawyers preparing bundles of documents that the mediator will not use.

Where you are represented, for the advocate the task of identifying minimum key documents becomes very important. You will need to focus on those items vital to establish the background - limiting the statements of case or other case management material to only those documents needed to understand the issues - and those necessary for you to establish your case or undermine that of your opponent. All non-essential documents should be rejected. This means that correspondence between the parties is seldom to be included unless you consider it absolutely crucial. If there are a large number of documents consider whether a reading list will assist the mediator.

The primary purpose of the documents is not to prove your case but to support the explanation of the issues that you are presenting to the other side. In considering what to include, see whether the issues appear to be clear to your opponent: parties sometimes surprise you at a very late stage of proceedings by their obvious misunderstanding of each other's position. This is particularly true of the way damages are calculated or argued. Documents that you wish to rely on in supporting your case on quantum should be furnished to the other side well in advance of the mediation hearing. Anything else can be brought with but is unlikely to be needed.

One warning to the minimal documents rule applies, and that is the production and use of expert reports in the mediation. For scientific or technical matters it may be essential for the mediator to develop a working understanding of the problem at hand and the issues dividing the parties, and not possible for him or her to do so in the absence of such reports. You need to consider whether such reports concern peripheral matters and do not, in fact, go to the core of the dispute between the parties; or whether there are adequate paths to settlement without the mediator or the parties having to consider or resolve the issues for expert evidence which would otherwise have to be proven or disproven at a trial. If it is vital that the mediator deals with the issues being addressed by experts, decide whether a report which may have been prepared for trial is too long or complex, and whether a summary or abstract might suffice. If you adopt this course do not forget that there may be additional documents needed, which are necessary to support the expert opinion upon which you wish to rely.

There will be instances where you have to decide whether the mediator should be asked to read the witness statements, if any. You may be better off preparing short summaries of what, it is anticipated, each witness will deal with at the trial. Mediators are unlikely to see the need to read witness statements prepared for trial. However you must force the issue if you consider it sufficiently important, and cost effective, bearing in mind at all times that you have to prove nothing to the mediator other than that you are prepared to negotiate a settlement; this, presumably, from a position of strength. Ultimately it is for you to decide or agree what the mediator ought to have. He may require very little, but you must be confident in asserting what you feel he really needs to see in order to understand the dispute, whether statements of case, core submissions, core documents, an abstract of the witness evidence or full experts' reports.

There may be confidential documents that you wish the mediator to see but not your opponent. These may be sent separately to the mediator prior to the hearing or shown to him in private session, marked as confidential for the mediator only.

It is in your interest to try to agree the minimum documents with your opposing number wherever possible. If you can reach an agreement on the contents of hearing bundles, a timetable, and the format and length of case summaries this should create a momentum and general spirit of agreement in which the participants arrive at the mediation in the right frame of mind.

Who should attend?

At an early stage you will need to consider whether you actually need legal representation at the mediation, even where you have been represented beforehand. For family and community mediations, ODR and telephone mediations, lawyers are usually absent. For civil/commercial disputes it is entirely a matter for the parties.

There will be few occasions when you conclude that representation is unnecessary but they may occur, for example if you are an experienced professional or, if you are the company secretary or the legal or financial director. You may decide that for reasons of strategy and cost, you consider yourself strong enough and competent enough to protect your own commercial interests should be permitted to attend without recourse to assistance.

You need, in that case, to have a thorough understanding of the procedure, the likely course of the negotiations, and the arguments and methods of persuasion likely to be adopted by the mediator.

If representation is necessary you should decide what the legal team should comprise. A sizeable legal team can undermine the economy of the process, and the opposite party may find it intimidating. The plenary and caucus rooms may suffer undue overcrowding. You may even convey the wrong message: you may inadvertently overemphasise the importance to you either of the dispute itself or your need to settle.

Undoubtedly there may be observers and support staff. City law firms are particularly gregarious and never seem to arrive without at least a small army of assistants. While the mediation process is a useful exercise for trainees and pupil barristers to observe, ideally attendance should be kept to a minimum. Always have the courtesy to ask in advance who may attend since the presence of unnecessary people may, at the least, have an impact on logistics. Where you intend to turn up with a large team you should agree this in advance with the mediator.

Barristers should be employed if they have had extensive contact with the dispute as prior litigation, or if it is likely they will conduct the trial should the mediation fail: this will enable counsel to gain knowledge of the nuances of the case he or she might not grasp from the papers, a feel for potential witnesses, and an insight into the lay client on the other side and his legal team. Counsel should also be engaged if he has particular specialist knowledge of the legal area of the dispute, experience as a mediation advocate or a particular relationship with any client involved (e.g. insurers). The flexibility of the process is such that counsel may be instructed without the attendance of a solicitor. In most smaller cases it will not be cost effective for counsel to attend.

There are a few rare occasions when the party himself does not have to attend. Such an instance may concern the defendant to a class action in the latter stages of a series of mediations dealing with similar subject matter but different claimants, by which time the defendant's negotiating position and range is already known. Usually, however, the client will attend either as an individual, or as a team that has the relevant knowledge, power to settle, and includes the core personalities involved in the dispute, and has directors or officers of equal importance to the other side.

The mediator will require the attendance of all parties necessary to effect a settlement of both the issue at hand and any relevant parallel or wider issues. You must consider with care (yourself, or with your lawyer,) who needs to attend. Despite strong legal advice as to who should be present, not all parties will be able to send a representative with full authority to settle: for example, an innovative solution, which addresses a wider settlement arena than the immediate dispute, may require authority from a director or a board resolution.

Common problems to bear in mind

It may be that a company's finance director is not present and the need for his presence was not envisaged when the mediation commenced. A local authority may need the approval of its finance or treasury committee based on an advice that the settlement is appropriate. A common occurrence is where insurers may be involved and present at the mediation but the insured parties may wish to be discreet about the participation of insurers, or the level of their cover, or the impact of the proposed settlement upon an insurer's confidential reserve. Often if the proposed settlement is complex it may need to have underlying financial arrangements agreed between banks or guarantors. Parties need to be mindful of these possibilities well in advance of the mediation. It will not surprise the experienced mediator to learn at some point during the day that authority to settle is not infinite. However steps must be taken to ensure that authority for any reasonably envisaged settlement is present.

Those individuals who attend the mediation because of their participation in the dispute (rather than its resolution) are not witnesses as such, but tend to be regarded in much the same way. Lawyers still regard mediation as a quasi-trial rather than a managed settlement negotiation, and feel the need to invite the attendance of those who will be witnesses at the trial if the mediation does not succeed. Normally it is not necessary to have those involved with the facts in issue - indeed a resolution can be easier to achieve if they are not involved in mediation - unless they are the principal parties. It is better not to have too many people in attendance. Ideally those attending should be the parties themselves, and, where necessary, a senior representative of a company or entity with authority to settle and/or the insurer. The mediator should be told who will be in attendance and their respective status.

There are other factors to take into account. You must consider with care any personality conflicts of which you are aware. There may be managerial or other same side conflicts for the mediator to bear in mind. A common example is the impact of the analysis of his decision-making on the person who made the decision being complained of. If he is likely to become aggressive or embarrassed if found wrong - will this impact upon the mediation, particularly his desire to settle or have his company settle? The party representatives must find the means to remove any potential undercurrent of conflict in the same side before it occurs.

The use of experts at the mediation needs careful thought. There may be fundamental, technical, valuation, tax or accounting issues, the last three being common. Both you and the mediator will want to ensure parity in the use of experts in the sense that neither party should be disadvantaged by imbalance in the use of expert evidence. All expert evidence to be relied upon, even if incomplete or in draft form, should be exchanged before the date of the mediation. Surprises are not conducive to settlement - they will merely cause the other side to walk out. So both sides must know experts are to attend the mediation, their identity and field of expertise, why they are coming and what they will say. Agreement may need to be reached about whether experts or advisers should attend or be on standby to be called if necessary, or to attend by telephone or videoconference.

Who Should Be Contactable?

Having a support team at your own or the solicitor's offices is very useful. Often during the course of the day, new information or documents can be required which may suddenly become vital during the latter stages of the mediation. These may relate to issues of liability or quantum, or to deal with the workability or impact of creative solutions. It may also be preferable to have interested third parties, for example the insurer, your accountant or a conveyancer available to provide telephone instructions rather than be present at the mediation. Please remember that mediations may continue long after office hours and if a support team or third party contact is required out of hours arrangements must be made accordingly.

Can I contact the mediator before the appointment?

You can or you may be telephoned by the mediator in advance of the appointment. A mediator, unlike a judge, can and frequently does contact each side separately beforehand, as he or she wishes. In training, mediators are encouraged to do so.

The mediation process does not start on the day of the mediation itself. Most substantial cases will benefit from a preliminary meeting between the mediator and the lawyers involved, or at least an exchange of telephone calls. It is perfectly possible for the mediator to see parties separately in advance should he choose to do so. This is particularly the case where he wants to get an early feel for the players involved, start building a rapport, particularly with the lawyers, or "pick up" on sticky issues or difficult people. Mostly a telephone call will suffice. This is intended as the beginning of a constructive, co-operative process in which the mediator will outline the process and responsibilities of the participants, check the lawyer's mediation experience, confirm who will be in attendance, request such further information as may be necessary, ask how the claim might settle, confirm that settlement authority exists, explore any existing offers, and generate a broader discussion of any likely pitfalls or hindrances to settlement. This information, or the nuances contained in some aspects of it, cannot necessarily be picked up from documents.

The mediator is not restricted to speaking merely to the lawyers involved. He or she may wish to speak directly with those holding authority to settle in order to start an empathic relationship, or to explain the procedure. This illustrates the flexibility of the process in which you are engaged. It also demonstrates that your mind set needs to be open and curious. Be prepared for your lawyer to be defensive about any direct approach to you as the client, since the lawyer will be concerned about the possibility of his losing control over the management of you and your case, which is an essential feature of the lawyer/client relationship during litigation, particularly for an advocate.

Making early contact after the mediator is appointed is also your opportunity to demonstrate to him a co-operative attitude. You will need to agree procedural matters with him or her, for example, the timetable for agreeing core documents, a list of issues, and the exchange of case summaries with the other side. Ask him whether you need to send him anything in advance. Make sure he has everything he needs. This begins a process of trust and confidence-building since you will have to trust him to treat all parties equally.

There are a number of common questions that a mediator might ask ahead of the mediation, the answers to which you will be expected to know. For example:

- Why has the dispute not settled so far?

- What concerns do either of you have about negotiating with the other side - i.e. why have you chosen to mediate rather than negotiate directly?

- What problems are likely to arise in mediation negotiations?

- What is required of the other side in order to bring about a satisfactory settlement at the mediation?

- What for you are the consequences of success?

- And what for you are the consequences of failure?

These are all matters that will assist the mediator to plan ahead, and to an extent force the parties each to reflect on their present position.

The ability to approach the mediator directly is a useful strategic tool. It enables you to provide confidential documents and information to him; to explain issues the way you see them; to feed through ideas as to how you think the case might settle; or to indicate your attitude. (If you are sending a confidential briefing note to the mediator this should contain a header or footer stating in terms that it is confidential to the mediator only.) You can also tell the mediator of previous negotiations and offers.

DECISIONS AS TO STRATEGY

The Role of Attendees

Before attending the mediation you must have a good understanding not only of your own role but that of everyone present. However strong you think your case is, and however much you wish to protect your interests - to the extent of protecting yourself from what you consider being a bad deal in the context of your legal rights - you need to recognise and support the philosophy and objectives of the mediation. Once you attend there is no room for personal cynicism about the process in which you are engaged. Nor will it assist for you to compare the progress of the mediation with that of a trial. If you are unprepared for what is to follow your expectations will be seriously challenged, and may be undermined.

In mediation you must understand your central participatory role in the process (rather than that of the lawyers) and be ready to:

- Speak and be heard in open and closed sessions. This is central to the dynamic of mediation, even though your lawyer may want to avoid the risk of losing control of you.

- Be aware of your levels of expectation and optimism, which may diminish during the day. Seek the support of others, including, where appropriate, the mediator himself.

- Focus on your interests as opposed to legal rights. Look at the wider picture for settlement options - the legal case should remain just a frame of reference, but settlement need not follow the legal case if your true interests are wider or you needs can be met elsewhere i.e. trading out of a dispute may be much more efficient and satisfactory than fighting it.

- Be able to discuss the reality of your situation.

- Try to promote positive solutions

- Keep open lines of communication in the face of challenging emotions and mistrust, strong feelings, grievances, and issues of credibility

- Do not allow your feelings get the better of you

- Ensure that the momentum is maintained during periods when your side is not in private session with the mediator as he deals with another party.

Your role, and that of anyone attending on your behalf, should be equally well defined prior to arriving at the venue. You must work out in advance who is going to do what, and the effect of your actively participating rather than just sitting and listening throughout the proceedings, as would be the case at a trial. Decide who will make the opening statement and do not assume that automatically it should be your lawyer or other representative as the advocate. Tactically you can use emotion to embarrass the other side or impress on them how sympathetically a judge might react at the trial to receiving your evidence. This can be an effective way of showing yourself as a good witness or emphasising favourable facts. A personal injury case may in particular require a demonstration of the nature of the disability, and this can be of considerable impact if shown by someone who will clearly be a good witness.

In any event your active participation will be your day in court, and this is the opportunity to give vent to feelings about the matter in a controlled but otherwise unrestricted way.

The opening remarks can be split between advocate and client, or even advocate, client and expert. Whatever the decision, the division of active roles should be planned well in advance and the contents well prepared.

As to the role of experts who are asked to be present, it is quite likely the mediator will have in mind how they should be used. He will probably ask experts to meet privately and separately, after any contribution they may have made in open session, and produce some jointly agreed parameters which can be used on a without prejudice basis to assist settlement strategies.

It is understandable if you may wish just to sit and listen, and take no active role until encouraged to do so by the mediator. An experienced mediator will know how to draw the parties into active participation, and sometimes on a level that may make the lawyers feel superfluous, although they must do their best to stifle that feeling if progress is obviously being made towards a resolution of the dispute.

Preparing the Attendees

It follows from the foregoing suggestions that it is advisable that, where you are represented, you have a pre-mediation conference with your lawyer or mediation advocate to understand precisely what mediation involves. You should assemble all of the information necessary for your representatives to understand not only the dispute but also any commercial or wider interests that require protection or advancement. At the conference you and your legal team can then begin to consider how you wish to negotiate. To that end at least one decision maker must be involved at the earliest stages of preparation. It is important to establish the difference between 'needs' and 'wants.'

The opportunity should also be taken to determine the difference between your *best alternative to a negotiated agreement* (*'BATNA'*) and your *worst alternative to a negotiated agreement* (*'WATNA'*).

A detailed risk analysis is a good way to prepare for both negotiations and to reduce expectations, particularly those held by persons in a higher managerial, corporate or institutional tier than those personally involved with the facts in dispute, and to diffuse any previously held aggressive or other strong emotions. Your lawyer should apply rigorous logic when comparing the litigation risk with any proposed commercial solution.

The advocate should also take the time to explain the tactics that a mediator might employ in relation to the parties, their lawyers and their experts. He must ascertain exactly what technical or legal assistance will be required.

You must appreciate, and make aware to all who are to attend, that normally a mediation can be a very long day. Any movement towards settlement is initially very slow, and it may take a long time to start. The momentum tends to pick up as the day ends but there can be large obstructions over small issues near the end of a concluded settlement, and these may run well into the evening. In addition any agreement reached must be reduced to writing and signed by the parties before they leave. Everyone should know that it is quite common for this stage to be long after nightfall, including well after the last train or normal bus home.

To that end legal representatives should not undermine the process by announcing that they have tickets for the Emirates and will be leaving at 5.00 pm. It is unprofessional, and potentially an act bringing their profession into disrepute. Experienced advocates are aware that mediation appointments are usually not time limited and should certainly make no other professional or social arrangements following a mediation. If that is your choice, so be it, but it should not be your lawyer's.

Unlike litigation there are no strictures on formal rehearsal or the training of parties for what is in store. A useful exercise to conduct for a very high value claim is to bring together everyone involved in the dispute and divide them into two teams to rehearse the entire negotiation strategy, with one team arguing for you and the other against. Be curious about the other side's bargaining position. Do not assume you know their view of the strengths and weaknesses of their case, or their underlying interests. You are unlikely to know anything of their personalities. But you can try and put yourself in their position to ascertain their needs and interests.

You must keep an open mind about the process and its likely outcome, and therefore be flexible about your expectations. These should not be absolute; you should have a negotiating range not a fixed position. The same can be said for each of the participants on your side, particularly insurers. Getting the participants into the right frame of mind is part of the mediation advocate's task. If there is travel involved in getting to the venue, perhaps a relaxed dinner in the hotel the night before would be a good idea.

HOW DO I DEAL WITH THE MEDIATOR?

Ethics and Other Matters

There are a number of other matters of which you should be aware, apart from dispute-specific items, and it may be important to discuss these in a pre-mediation conference with your representative. These concern aspects of your relationship with your opponent, and with the mediator. Your solicitor or counsel will know how to conduct themselves professionally since there are rules laid down by the governing or regulatory bodies of their profession. If the mediation takes place against the backdrop of existing litigation, the advocate's approach and conduct is governed by the Civil Procedure Rules 1999 (and particularly the Overriding Objective under Part 1), specific case management directions, and his or her obligations to the Court which are sustained by sanctions. What this means in simple terms, is that just because a mediation is not a trial in court, your lawyer will not knowingly lie to the mediator, or to the other side, on your behalf nor permit you to do so, nor stand by while you do. Do not ask him or her to do so. Do not expect to keep your advocate if he or she knows that you are misleading the mediator or the other side.

This is not simply a matter of moral high ground. Should you achieve a settlement it will operate under the law of contract. If the contract is founded upon a misrepresentation, it can be set aside by the Court, irrespective of the fact that it was made during the course of mediation, and irrespective of the confidentiality attaching to the process.

The only rules directly governing a mediation are those contained in the mediation agreement or otherwise agreed between the parties and the mediator as a matter of procedure. There are no rules of evidence. Your advocate is engaged to protect or enhance your interests in settling the dispute by whatever means he may consider expedient, professional and proper. This freedom may conflict with the extent to which either he, on instructions, or you are completely candid with the mediator or with the other side in presenting your case or negotiating stance. The ethical dilemma for lawyers is still something of a grey area and the subject of some ongoing debate, however the bottom line is that conduct during a mediation, which brings the reputation of a profession into disrepute, is likely to attract a disciplinary sanction.

For practical purposes, when thinking about or discussing in conference the tactical approach to adopt in the forthcoming negotiation, either with the opposite party or the mediator, it is as well to keep in mind the following:

(i) The mediator succeeds because he operates on the basis of a relationship of trust. Each party reposes their trust in him, and he for his part must assume that what he is told, particularly what he is told in confidence, or is told to advance to the other side, is truthful. A breakdown of trust in the mediator is likely to cause the mediation to fail. Should you break faith with him he will find it difficult to continue to represent your position to the other parties. The mediation will end.

(ii) If the opposing party is unhappy or uncomfortable or aggrieved at your negotiating style or position, he may simply walk away at any time. This is very likely if your opponent believes you to be disingenuous.

(iii) As I have said above, and reiterate because of its importance, mediated agreements may be set aside by the courts for being induced by misrepresentation in the same way as any other contract, with all the consequences that will necessarily flow from such an eventuality.

Authority to Settle

It is an essential requirement of the process that all sides come to the mediation with authority to settle, and the mediation agreement will usually specify that this is so. *All persons who have to approve the settlement* should ordinarily be present at the mediation session, and where the settlement is subject to approval by a higher authority, that higher authority must attend and see the process, otherwise he will not be affected by the dynamic which propels the parties towards the agreement: any party external to the mediation may need to be persuaded that the settlement figure is justified. This means the parties themselves have authority, and not just their legal advisers, unless the latter are fully authorised to settle.

Your lawyer will probe you in advance about any limit of your authority to settle and you should be prepared for this. The mediator may well wish to receive a formal acknowledgement from your lawyer that his authority extends to the full amount of the Claim. If in fact the settlement authority is limited, you should ensure that the limit extends at least beyond offers previously made and rejected. The mediator may also require specific information about settlement authority to be given from third parties, an obvious example being an insurer's reserve.

Your representative can not discharge his duty, will certainly ensure the mediation shall fail, and may well be guilty of professional misconduct, if:

1. he fails to come to mediation with appropriate authority e.g. the decision-maker does not attend, or his authority is wholly inadequate and he fails to advise the mediator about authority problems;

2. he misrepresents to the mediator the level of his authority; or

3. he represents at the mediation he has no authority as a tactic to buy time or to impose negotiation pressure on the other side.

A mediation advocate must never overlook authority issues, and therefore you must give him or her the information required in the form he or the mediator requires. Even if you are confident about your authority to settle, towards the end of the mediation the considerable and perhaps unexpected movement that often takes place can be derailed by one side lacking necessary authority. The settlement itself may easily be jeopardised. Therefore if you cannot make sure that you have the means to meet a settlement because the momentum of the process is running away and there may be some circumstance where it is not possible to obtain authority e.g. your board's approval is required, at least indicate in good faith when the authority will be made available, come clean about the problem as early as possible, and have the courage to suspend the proceedings if you judge it necessary to do so.

How do I prepare my interest statement?

It has generally come to be regarded as an essential feature of pre-mediation preparation that representatives for each party exchange with the others and send to the mediator in good time for the mediation day a reasonably concise statement of their client's case and the submissions that they wish to make. If you are unrepresented you may still be asked by the mediator to provide in writing a document setting out the claim or dispute, your needs and interests, the arguments you wish to advance, and details of how you see settlement. Some of the information can remain confidential should you wish.

The purpose of this document is really threefold: first, to inform the mediator and your opposing party of the live issues in dispute and your current position; second, to explain and justify the merits of your stance; and third, as a vehicle towards settlement, indicating a willingness to make appropriate concessions and pointing up settlement options. Tell the mediator about your needs and interests.

In spite of the need for brevity you will wish to take advantage of the opportunity to make sufficient key points in the written statement to persuade the mediator and the other side of the strengths of the case as seen from your own viewpoint. Your opponent will probably read it before the mediation hearing, and, like any piece of effective written advocacy, it should aim to overwhelm the opposing party and deflate his expectation. Therefore you should establish the key evidence in support of your case, explain why it has force, and why at trial you are likely to succeed on the merits. Although you need to prove nothing at the mediation, your ability to do so at trial is likely to be the platform from which you build negotiating strength. You should identify your approach to settlement, rehearse the risks, and can even make an offer or indicate possible concessions.

It is therefore clear that some skill is needed in the preparation of this document. It is more astute to direct it at your opposing lay party, since it may be the first time this information will have been received without the interference of their lawyers.

I suggest that your Interest Statement should follow the template:

The Position Statement

1. Identify the Parties *and* the Participants

The mediator does not necessarily know who everyone is, or his or her status. Provide a list of the key personalities he will need to know about and their involvement in the subject matter of the dispute. For ease of reference he may prefer this to be in alphabetical order. This should not be confined to the parties to litigation, or indeed the parties to the dispute. It should extend to anyone having an influence over the outcome, which may include spouses or relatives of individuals, and directors or managers of corporate or institutional parties.

2. The Relevant History

Set out in concise form the relevant history leading up to the dispute. Concise in this instance means what it says - tell the mediator only what he needs to know. This should include any court intervention, finding or relevant part-disposal of any contentious matter.

3. Outline the Dispute

This is a key part of the document. Identify the issues that comprise the whole dispute, or are contextually relevant. Set out those matters that are agreed, not agreed and each party's views.

4. Your Case

Set out your case both as to facts and law, and the nature and extent of the claims as to quantum. (If this is a personal injury claim you should attach an updated schedule of loss.) Identify, as required, those matters of fact and law in dispute between the parties. Where appropriate explain your feelings. Show why your case on the contested issues is likely to be preferred by a court were the matter to be tried.

5. The Gateway to Settlement

Identify those issues or claims that you believe are capable of being resolved. Explain why you agreed to mediation. Deal with any previous settlement history and prior or current offers. Indicate what you hope to achieve by the mediation - what are your legal, commercial and personal objectives. Do not close the door to settlement by setting at this stage any limits or pre-conditions. Be constructive and try to dispel any prior aggression.

6. A Chronology

If the mediator requests one, or if you believe having one may assist the mediator, prepare a chronology. Such a document should be neutral and avoid positional statements, and if possible should be agreed. It should be short and concise providing the key dates and a succinct explanation of major events where necessary. It may help to reduce the number of factual disputes between the parties.

HOW DO I PREPARE FOR THE MEDIATION DAY/S?

What do I want to achieve?

Your preparation should at least make you understand precisely what outcome you need, not just in relation to the legal cause of action or defence, but taking into account the full range of your wider commercial, relationship, personal and emotional interests where present. One effective way of doing this is to list out everything you are interested in achieving and then prioritising these by dividing them into categories. I suggest that the categories be ranked 'needs' 'would like' 'nice to have' and the items within each category ranked with a value, so they are all prioritised within each category [see Figure 1]. Once the list has been compiled with values attached, it is a useful exercise to anticipate the other side's list, attributing such values as you believe are appropriate. The differences in value will give rise to bargaining, with hopefully, each side having matters to which they attribute less value being available to trade, with the recipient attributing greater value in their hands [see Figure 2]. A similar approach may be to compile in advance matters/items/ issues that might be given away.

Fig. 1 Preparation of a prioritised List of Needs and Interests

Own Client	Client's Perception of Other Side's view of Us	Client's perception of Other Side	Other Side Actual (Discover at Mediation)
We need	They think we need	We think they need	They need
1.	1.	1.	1.
2.	2.	2.	2.
3.	3.	3.	3.
4.	4.	4.	4.
We Would Like	They think we would like	We think they would like	They Would Like
5.	5.	5.	5.
6.	6.	6.	6.
7.	7.	7.	7.
8.	8.	8.	8.
Happy to have	They think we might want	We think they might want	They're happy to have
9.	9.	9.	9.
10.	10.	10.	10.
11.	11.	11.	11.
12.	12.	12.	12.

This notion of looking for 'differences' which may be traded is a common strategy of the mediator, and your position may best be advanced by using the mediator to ascertain the true values within the other side's list. An experienced mediator will use this process, but not reveal such information.

Fig. 2 Preparation of a prioritised Bargaining List for Negotiation

Own Client	Client's Perception of Other Side's view of Us
We will give	They think we will give
1. 2. 3. 4.	1. 2. 3. 4.
We might give	They think we might give
5. 6. 7. 8.	5. 6. 7. 8.
We will not give	They think we will not give
9. 10. 11. 12.	9. 10. 11. 12.

Single issue cases (i.e. arguments solely about a sum of money to be paid) should be broken down into smaller items: a payment of money as the single issue can be divided into several issues by the application of time, so that it includes having to consider and agree the amount, the nature of the payment, for example a single transfer or tranches; if the latter, how many and over what period; any discounting for early payment; any interest; any provision for default; provision for costs; any confidentiality attaching to the settlement. Thus what appears to be a sole issue can be converted into eight, for the purpose of bargaining.

It will be plain by now from the tenor of this book that mediation is not merely a negotiating process that requires little or no preparation. Do not assume that the mediation hearing will merely be a horse-trading session. It follows from the preceding section that your case must be mastered and prepared so that you can meet difficult questions about it, put not only by the other side but also by the mediator.

You need to understand why everyone present is there, and how these can help you. Consider why you are going – to be seen to be right, such as in Court? Or because being right isn't enough, and the Court cannot actually help you, win or lose.

- Do not have absolute expectations - your case will be the subject of reality testing both by the mediator in private meetings, or caucuses, and by the other side in open or plenary sessions.

- Know what you want to achieve in terms of priorities: you must be comfortable with what is essential and not what is an ideal, whether a monetary settlement or otherwise.

- You may have to deal with the realities of the situation as these may change during the mediation; otherwise you may face winning a Pyrrhic victory.

- You can (and should) treat the mediation as your 'day in court', participating actively to make all the points about which you are concerned.

- The ambit of settlement options is not constrained by either strict legal merits or litigation procedure, and you can look elsewhere for goals you want to achieve, including non-monetary goals, and matters outside the present dispute.

- Procedurally, there is a possibility that separate meetings may occur within the mediation, e.g. between the two lawyers only, or the experts, lay clients, accountants, or directors as the mediator considers appropriate and the parties agree.

Advice on Mediation

If you or your company need written advice from your lawyer concerning the mediation this should be focused on all matters relevant to you, not just the legal case. You need to provide full instructions concerning your aspirations, which may go substantially beyond what you consider your lawyer might want to know. You are really seeking advice against which you can make a commercial decision during the mediation - whether or not to accept any potential offer, or how much to offer yourself. In this respect you need firm advice from the lawyer about what will happen should there be no settlement. You need a firm indication of litigation risk, and an accurate forecast of the legal costs and disbursements involved, including recoverability if winning, and liability if losing.

At the legal level of the dispute, you will need to provide as much information as your solicitor, and perhaps counsel, will need to assess the cause of action or defence in terms of its merits and quantum. To that end you will assist with all the facts of the case, the evidence available, the quantum of damage likely to be recovered, and any other relief required, including its enforceability. You need to have your lawyer evaluate the best and worst case outcomes and what percentage chance of each is probable. You may wish to factor in any available choice of process or particular timescale.

Unlike an advice purely for litigation, you will have to explain where appropriate any commercial or personal level to the dispute. Your representative must understand what commercial arrangement reflects your needs and interests, and see what, if any, commercial solutions are available and suitable that might take into account past and future business opportunities involving the parties.

There is also likely to be a personal level to the dispute that may be of great importance to you, since unlike litigation, mediation offers the prospect of   personal closure and moving on with your life. You are not able to secure one of the benefits of a litigated outcome - in court you may have the satisfaction of a judge saying you are right, although conversely you risk the court's disapproval of your actions, or you may win or lose only on a legal technicality. To resolve any personal issues you need a process of catharsis, and experienced mediators will be alive to this and use it as a path to settlement.

To advise properly upon the conduct and potential outcome of the litigation your lawyer must have a clear view of what you want to achieve. Is a monetary settlement all you want? What are your priorities? What objectives are essential and what are an ideal? You will have to deal with the realities of the situation so you must know what these are, and in doing so you will come to see what range of proposals your advocate can make.

You want your lawyer to be part of a team which is designed to put your interests first. Unless he is highly experienced at mediation, his innate training may be an impediment because he is drawn to thinking only about the legal aspects of the dispute.

The mediator will assist you by ensuring the lawyer

- Keeps an open mind about the process;

- Understands the process is not like litigation; it is to secure an outcome both sides can live with, rather than creating a 'winner' and a 'loser'.

- Learns about the procedure;

- Is prepared in all aspects of your case;

- Understands that the legal framework of the dispute may be only one aspect of the parties' interests;

- Is receptive to solutions which are outside the legal framework of the dispute;

- Uses the mediator as a tool with which to obtain a benefit for you, rather than sees him as an obstacle.

Mediation is designed to give you control of your problem. The holistic, healing approach with which mediation is concerned is intended to help you find a desirable solution to it, and enable you to draw a line and move on with your life.

Checklist for final preparation

Any checklist should include the following steps:

1. Review all the files and know what evidence supports your case: who are the witnesses, what are the core documents, do you have expert reports and real evidence? Ensure you have all the information necessary for a final evaluation of the case.

2. Know what heads of damage are claimed: is your calculation justified and supported for each?

3. Prepare calculations of interest from when the claim accrued down to the mediation, and then to an expected trial date.

4. Know (if appropriate) what assertions of law are to be advanced

5. List out the particular strengths and weaknesses in your case.

6. List out the particular strengths and weaknesses in your opponent's case.

7. Set out the costs to date of your own side, the expected costs of the other side, and the anticipated costs of both parties from here to the end of the trial. Make sure you go into the mediation knowing your breakdown of costs to date and any revisions to costs budgets, and calculate the likely irrecoverable element. Get the mediator to have the other side produce theirs, since it is vital he knows what they are.

8. Review the mediation procedure - know what to expect.

9. Confirm the attendance of all necessary participants involved in the mediation, and that the necessary authority to settle is available - the dispute cannot settle otherwise

10. Mull over your negotiation strategy and refine it: know what compensation or restitution is possible; what

plans for future action are practicable; how emotional or psychological issues can be dealt with; and how to 'expand the pie' by identifying opportunities that will be of benefit to both sides, e.g. costs savings, tax savings, time and opportunity cost savings, restoration or preservation of commercial, social or family relationships.

11. Consider whether the settlement aimed for has any necessary financial, tax or technical implications that might give rise either to authority problems or potentially cause a settlement agreement to be delayed.

12. Prepare a draft settlement agreement on the terms that you are hoping for. This will be useful to the mediator in the negotiation stage.

13. Ensure that you have available everything that you will need on the day of the mediation:

(a) calculator

(b) lap-top computer

(c) mobile phone

(d) important contact numbers

(e) case summaries/position statements

(f) agreed documents bundle

(g) other documents to be made available if referred to

(h) schedule of damages

(i) interest calculation

(j) costs breakdown

(k) note of opening statement

(l) draft agreement including, where appropriate, draft confidentiality clause.

THE MEDIATION DAY

What can I expect?

In the UK civil/commercial mediation model most mediation hearings last a day. Complex or multi-party cases may last two or three days, but even in very high value claims it would be unusual for a mediation to last for much longer. This contrasts with the model used by Family Mediators in this jurisdiction, which are based on a series of fixed appointments which may last a period of weeks, and in which there is very little if any private caucusing.

Commercial time limited mediation schemes can last for four or five hours and be fixed by agreement. In such cases the time is usually only fixed in relation to the mediator's or mediation service provider's fee, which may be topped up at an hourly rate thereafter.

Do not expect the mediation will finish within the set time frame: it is notoriously difficult to concertina the time required for the process to succeed to the satisfaction of the parties into a mere three hours.

Make sure of the due date and time, familiarise yourself with the location of the mediation, and ensure that you arrive on time. If you are visiting an unfamiliar venue allow time to park, and to unload and carry any necessary files and materials to the venue. Being late sends a wrong message. If possible arrive a little early to meet the mediator and establish a base in the room in which the mediator informs you your private sessions will be conducted.

Although you will have burdened the mediator beforehand with as little as possible, take with you to the mediation all files, and copies of any documents intended for the other side, and writing materials. If you are going to produce documents to the other side that they have not yet seen, hand them out after any explanation you need to give, not beforehand.

Mediations commonly run well into the night, and certainly after close of normal business hours. Being under pressure of time impacts on the settlement dynamics - either you feel you must leave, or the pressure of time makes the settlement ultimately unsatisfactory when considered with hindsight. Therefore make sure you put enough time in your schedule: do not fix afternoon meetings or conferences; do not expect to get away for social activities in the early evening. Beware of the possible length of the appointment and come prepared for a very long day.

Even when agreement has been reached it may still take some time for a document incorporating the heads of agreement to be prepared. The mediator will not allow the lawyers to depart without having done so, since he will not risk the settlement becoming unraveled if the parties have second thoughts on the way home. If you have no legal representation, the mediator may draft very general heads of terms and advise you to go to a neutral lawyer simply to have the details drawn up.

> Allow for substantial periods of inactivity during the day when the mediator may be elsewhere and you have completed any tasks set for you in his or her absence. You should constantly finesse your negotiating position, adapting to any additional information or change affecting you. You may want to bring something else to do, or to read. You should not, but it is understandable.

Procedure

Although a key feature of mediation is its flexibility, where the parties are free to choose their own procedure with the guidance of the mediator, a standard procedure has now evolved so that mediators and mediation advocates can be trained, and disputants can be told what the process usually entails.

Irrespective of the venue, the mediator is, in effect, the host. He or she will meet and greet the parties, explain the facilities and give guidance on the day's proceedings. This introductory meeting is important as it will usually be the first opportunity most of the participants have to meet the mediator. Some mediators take their time over these preliminary meetings, seeking information or clarification, engaging with the parties to start to build a relationship of confidence and trust, exploring the format of the opening joint session, and where necessary, encouraging or even cajoling reluctant parties to join and participate in that meeting.

The parties and their representatives will first be asked to read through and sign the mediation agreement, either in the privacy of their own rooms or at the commencement of the opening session. The mediator will then sign that document himself. This feature of private dispute processing is of itself unusual, since the mediator is likely to have been acting de facto under the terms of the mediation agreement for days, if not a few weeks, prior to its execution.

The Opening Joint Session or 'Plenary'

After the private room introductions, the parties will be invited to join the mediator together in an opening joint session. After everyone in the room has introduced themselves, the mediator will give a short introduction to the procedure and the approximate timetable in which he will explain his or her function. Most mediators will take this opportunity to explain a little of their own background and experience and make certain key points:

- That the process is voluntary and the parties are free to leave if they choose;

- That the entire process is confidential and without prejudice to the extent the law permits, and will remain so unless or until a settlement agreement is reached;

- That the contents of the private sessions are confidential and will not be disclosed to the other side unless the mediator is expressly permitted to do so;

- That the parties are expected to have settlement authority.

The mediator will also encourage the parties by acknowledging the progress they have made in merely attending; he will probably caution them not to read anything into his choice of the order in which he sees the parties privately or the relative length of any private sessions.

Essentially the open meeting is client-centred. The seating should be the mediator, then a lay client either side of him, and then the lawyers and outside of them any experts, supporting witnesses and observers, including third party decision makers. This is intended to contrast with litigation where in all hearings the lawyer is placed between the judge and the opposing parties.

The mediator will invite an opening statement of about 5 - 10 minutes from the legal representatives of each party followed by a short statement from each lay client. He will stress that these statements must be uninterrupted, and should be listened to carefully. The statements may result in a discussion. The mediator will generally summarise the parties' respective positions.

Although the opening plenary session is intended normally only to establish your current position it may turn into an open preliminary negotiating session, or subsequently you may find yourself in open negotiation. Persuasion at a joint meeting will require a balance between empathy and assertiveness - be neither aggressive nor submissive: you believe your interests are legitimate and valid; explain to the other side in the presence of the mediator those interests, needs and perspectives. Express an understanding of your opponent's argument, or at least a desire to understand. Be neither overtly sympathetic nor indicate agreement, but listen attentively and actively, looking for areas of potential mutual gain.

Try, if you can, to lay the foundation for problem solving - at the outset find a framework within which to negotiate as part of a reciprocal process that will allow both parties to emphasise their case and make the necessary assertions while at the same time avoid position-taking by identifying interests, needs, resources and capabilities. Do not evaluate what is said until later in private session where you can try to brainstorm suggestions as a problem solving exercise, but without asserting ownership of any ideas that may be produced, and keep your ambitions realistic.

After the opening session the parties retire to their separate rooms. The mediator will then move from room to room, speaking with the parties, until there is either resolution or deadlock. He explores with each party the strengths and weaknesses of its or their case and the quantum, risks, and costs implications. He will want to know each party's wider aspirations for a successful outcome, and try to assess what each regards as most important. Even if he is not evaluative, that is, even if he will not express an opinion on the merits of your position, the mediator is hardly passive. He will probe your contentions and expectations. At the end of each private session or caucus he will review what he has been told and clarify what he may reveal to the other side, including any offers. He will want to know about any previous settlement proposals and on what basis they were calculated and rejected.

The mediator may at some stage invite the parties to return to a joint open session, so that a direct explanation or presentation of a particular point can be made, and if there is a particular difficulty. He may fragment the parties' teams by having the experts, the lawyers, or the decision-makers meet entirely separately, either simultaneously or consecutively. On the other hand the mediator may decide for good reason to have no further joint meeting after the opening session.

The mediation will be concluded in one of three ways: there will be a concluded agreement; there will be an insuperable difficulty causing one or both sides to withdraw; or the time available may expire with the parties adjourning the mediation to be continued on another occasion.

Where there is a settlement the lawyers will draft the necessary agreement in as much detail as possible and those present with the requisite authority will sign it before leaving. If one or both of the parties withdraw the mediator may have to make a report to that effect to the mediation service provider or, where it is a court-annexed mediation, to the court. The mediator will only report the fact of failure and is not entitled to apportion blame or have the court investigate it.

If the time available for the appointment expires the parties may wish to assess whether there is sufficient momentum in the negotiations to continue on another occasion with or without the mediator. It may take a little time for you and your lawyers to assess the position. If the mediator is still required a further session should be arranged as soon as reasonably practicable after the first. In the family and Harvard mediation models a series of appointments are booked, rather than trying to conclude a settlement within a day.

The Opening Statement

Presenting the opening statement in mediation is unlike making opening submissions to a judge at trial. However strange it feels, the advocate should address the opposite party directly and not the mediator. If you are unrepresented remember that this is your one opportunity to talk about your concerns directly to the other side without interruption. At this early stage the aim is to provide information about your position in respect of the issues, not to negotiate or altercate or to propose or accept solutions.

Unlike a trial there is no formal structure. The mediator decides who goes first. Invariably it will be the claimant, but not always. Most importantly you should be aware that there is usually no right of reply, although unlike a court hearing the mediator will now customarily invite the parties to speak personally after or in addition to the lawyers.

Do not waste the opportunity presented by the invitation to give an opening statement: the mediator will ask the other side to listen to you without interruption, and focus on what you are saying. There are few opportunities in any contentious work involving dispute resolution processes to be able to address directly a decision maker on the other side without interruption. Make full use of it.

Prepare and, if you can, practice the opening statement before the session. This will aid conciseness and accuracy. Brevity is important. Be concise and business like. If you haven't before, introduce your supporters. Then provide an uncluttered, unemotional focus on the core issues, not minutiae, dealing with your current needs - not past obsessions or grievances. Do not include much history unless it is directly relevant to the present settlement process. Do not refer to documents unless you consider it absolutely vital to do so.

On the other hand, a visual aid, such as a chart or diagram, might hold the attention of the opposing side and make it easier to explain either a complicated or a technical position. At the commencement or conclusion you should assert your desire to work towards a settlement or some such positive statement (even if at that point you don't feel like it).

You will already have decided in advance who will be present at the first and any subsequent joint session. If it is tactically advantageous the lawyer will divide the presentation between those who should deal with the law, the facts, and emotive or technical issues. You may then be asked to deal with your commercial imperatives or emotional concerns, and can expect the mediator to encourage personal exchanges.

Letting you give vent to your feelings is what the mediator wishes to happen. You need to decide on their likely impact and potential importance. It may be the only time that you can say precisely what you want in the way you want to say it. You should be given the opportunity to express your version and understanding of events, unless your lawyer considers it would be disastrous for you to do so.

In preparing the contents of your opening statement consider each of the following items:

(i) How briefly to deal with the history of the matter: cut out all unnecessary detail; where possible focus on the present situation and the future rather than the past.

(ii) How to summarise the main points of the dispute between the parties as you see them, using broad themes: go over the facts of the case, indicating areas of agreement and disagreement and the available evidence. Explain your analysis of liability and damages based on the facts of the case; if you are responding, say why you disagree with your opponent's statement of case. Analyse any different levels at which the conflict operates, including substantive law and the risk to the respective parties in either commercial or personal terms against their desire to end the litigation.

(iii) How best to outline what you want to achieve in the mediation: avoid specific settlement figures at the outset and speak in general terms. Avoid emotive language but explain the impact of the dispute on you. Suggest what decisions need to be made at the mediation.

You will need to be realistic. While emphasising your strengths and presenting your case in the most favourable way, do not ignore its weaknesses. Tell the other side if you have already factored weaknesses into a previous offer, or at least that you are conscious of the weaker points of your case for the purpose of negotiation.

Select language and a style of presentation that will engage the opposing party in what you are saying - tell them that which will keep their attention - and do not cause them to switch off by telling them what they do not want to hear. Be positive - explain that you wish to have a settlement that will satisfy both sides.

After you have concluded your own presentation listen carefully and without interruption to what the other side are saying in their opening. Do not be dismissive. You may well be hearing something for the first time or something you have not appreciated or realised before. It is such revelations that break the logjam of previously held entrenched positions. If you are cynical about what you are hearing, try to ensure that you do not express such cynicism with facial or other gestures that are likely to alienate or antagonise the other side.

On the other hand be aware that the party opposite may not have a genuine interest in settlement, and may only be there to assess the strengths and weaknesses of your case, using the mediation as a tactical device within the litigation (at whatever risk to himself on costs). If you suspect this to be the case do not duck the issue, and raise it with the mediator in caucus early on. Ask for some tangible sign of goodwill and consider whether your best interests are served by remaining if you are not reassured.

Private and Open Sessions

I have already discussed the flexibility with which the mediator can manage the process, and the range of meetings he has open to him, particularly in a multi-party or multi-level dispute. There he may have a plenary meeting and then joint or group sessions, and deal with experts or lawyers or laymen in parallel or sequential meetings. Do not be a passive observer on the question of management. Make a constructive contribution as to how you think your interests will be best served. You can and should disagree with the mediator if you have a good reason for doing so.

Open Sessions

Having both conducted and heard the presentations in the initial open or plenary session you will be in a position to consider the advantages and disadvantages of such open sessions. Invariably the mediator will move from the opening session into private or 'caucus' sessions and rarely have another open session until settlement is achieved. He or she may utilise an open session to try and overcome a particularly difficult topic within the dispute where otherwise there is a complete logjam, the issue needs to be dealt with by the parties on a face to face basis, and the alternative is that one party or the other will leave. Occasionally either the advocate or the mediator may consider that conveying an explanation of a position or argument on a second hand basis will not be as effective as direct dialogue.

Try and gauge the impact of the first open meeting from its outset. Often it will be the first time you and your advisers have met for a while; sometimes you may not previously have met at all; certainly it will be the first occasion on which you and your team have an opportunity to hear what the other side is saying first hand, and see how they are likely to appear in court. This will enable you to form a view about the value of the open sessions.

The opportunity to make as much use of personal contact as possible is valuable, since one of the first things a solicitor will do in litigation is to keep the parties apart so that the process can be managed by lawyers. If you can restore the conflict to the level of personal ownership this may make institutional opponents, or insurers standing behind them, very uncomfortable. It also provides you with a clear sense of having your 'day in court'.

Closed Sessions

The private or closed session, or 'caucus' as it is sometimes called, is a central feature of the mediation process in the model most frequently used in the United Kingdom. One can do away with open meetings, including the joint opening session, and some mediators do; but you cannot do without caucusing, since this is probably the most effective dynamic in mediation. Curiously the continental model, used here in family mediation, does not ordinarily use caucusing and prefers the parties together all the time except for time-outs to seek advice.

In closed meetings the mediator holds a series of separate meetings with the parties in dispute. His or her aim is to bring the parties to a settlement by identifying hidden agendas and exploring problem solving proposals. The key is confidentiality. He will slowly build up trust, while at the same time offering the objective view of a neutral who is sympathetic to, but firm with, each party.

But the mediator may only divulge what he has learned from one party in a closed session if express permission is given. You must decide whether such permission should be given having first considered what, if any, impact such matters will have on the negotiation process. Sometimes the mediator will himself inform you that he would not advise disclosing a certain fact yet. On occasions he will hold the information ready to use when he thinks the time is right, which might be much later in the day, or may possibly remain unnecessary. There may be a conflict between you and your lawyer about such disclosure, which should properly only be resolved in the absence of the mediator.

The caucus sessions are initially quite lengthy, particularly the first with each side, which is essentially an information-gathering exercise. These private meetings tend to speed up during the day, particularly once offers are made. Typically both parties will maintain in the initial open session and the early caucuses a legalistic position based on what they perceive as their rights. As time passes and confidence in both the process and the mediator grows, solutions that are based on the best interest of the parties rather than strictly perceived legal rights become more acceptable.

There are various forms of separate or private meetings in which the mediator will have different objectives. He may wish to speak to you alone without the advice, influence or pressure from your lawyer. You should be prepared in advance to deal with such a proposal. Equally the mediator may wish to see all client parties together, but without their lawyers, to focus on commercial settlement options which might not necessarily reflect their strict legal interests. Or he may wish to see the lawyers for the opposing parties together without clients, to explore realistic settlement options where the parties are themselves proving intransigent, unrealistic in their expectations or problematic. In this case you must be particularly wary of your lawyer inadvertently breaching confidentiality, which belongs to you.

There are some common matters that are of concern in dealing with private sessions:

- Irrespective of which type of private meeting you become involved in, check the confidentiality position with the mediator at the end of each session.

- Avoid becoming over-anxious at the length of another party's separate meeting with the mediator.

- Be careful not to fall into the trap of misreading empathy by the mediator as a lack of neutrality.

- Try to use the mediator to obtain information from the other side that you may need to construct a settlement which may meet their needs.

- Do not get frustrated by what appears to be a lack of progress during private sessions, particularly in the early stages of the day.

- Make the best use of periods following a private session with mediator to reflect on what has gone on during it to re-evaluate the case, your strategy, and the options open to you.

The Role of the Advocate at the Mediation

Unlike the representative function of solicitor or counsel at a trial, the mediation advocate is not present principally to convey his client's case to the mediator and the other side. He has an equally important role as his client's adviser. He must protect his client's best interests, as he sees them, while at the same time trying to make the process work. Occasionally these responsibilities conflict. The advocate must constantly evaluate the case and its progress in the mediation. He must stand up to an over-zealous mediator, when necessary. And while focusing on his client's legal interests, he must think laterally if a solution is to be found to overcome resistance while accommodating his client's legal position. To that extent the mediation advocate must release the client from his control as the case manager and allow the mediator to investigate any wider agenda or needs, while at the same time using the legal case as a frame of reference with which to ascertain realistically the client's best and worst alternatives to a negotiated agreement.

Mediation is a team game. You, the client, must be included in the process from start to finish. This extends to preparing together during the mediation and taking advantage of quiet time outside caucus sessions to adjust negotiating strategy throughout. Thus, your lawyer should explain right through the day what is happening and why. This will help you relax and approach negotiations constructively. Your goals may change as information flows during the course of the mediation. Your lawyer has to keep analysing the perceived strengths and weaknesses of your case, and of your approach to settlement, as the position changes.

Unsurprisingly, the lawyer will concentrate on issues of fact and law. You, though, may well have issues that could be of crucial importance to you but outside matters the lawyer sees as strictly relevant.

When in joint session the advocate will usually either present the argument or support the decision-maker in presenting it. This will ensure that the joint meetings are concise, focused on real issues, and there is less risk of the mediation coming to an abrupt halt if a party reacts unfavourably to misgivings or emotions.

Your lawyer will want to avoid up-beat submissions, but express his or her confidence in the merits, balanced by an emphasis on attending the mediation in good faith and with the intention of finding a solution.

Advocacy during private sessions is equally different from trial work. A confrontational style is out of place. Consistent with defending your position, your lawyer's mind set should regard the dispute as a problem to be solved, not a conflict to be won. Therefore you should expect an experienced mediation advocate to adopt a constructive, problem solving approach, although the mediator must be persuaded of your points. Your lawyer may need to overcome the mediator in caucus because he exerts a powerful influence. Allow him as a neutral to act instinctively; but be prepared to have him go back to the plenary session, to meet the lawyers on the other side, assist technical experts in a session confined to their discipline, and above all to view the process flexibly. This includes allowing discussions between clients and, where different, between principal decision-makers. For a lawyer to let go of his client in this way is difficult, but it must be done, at the right time.

You will need to work closely with your lawyer throughout the negotiation process: he needs to be a friend and supporter to the decision-maker when times get tough. That can be a rare and emotive situation for the lawyer, particularly if counsel is being instructed. So your team should be active and use idle time creatively, considering the strengths and weaknesses of both sides as they change with the dynamic of the process. Consider inventive solutions as ways to overcome deadlock. Try to avoid entrenched positions; keep your temper under control, and think carefully about what happens next if you think of leaving.

Your lawyer will therefore be expected to know the legal case in some detail when he attends the mediation. He will also have to cater for a non-legal approach, sometimes from the outset, and particularly where you have a weak case in law.

He or she will know the documents. Even though there may only be a slim core bundle for the mediator, the lawyer should take all of your files, or understand where to reach any document it transpires you must have, which the mediator has not seen.

Often you may be required to answer a point raised by the other side and conveyed through the mediator.

Finally your lawyer will be required to draft the settlement agreement. This will be invariably as soon as the parties have come to terms, although he may advise you to start parts of it beforehand. The parties may not reach agreement at the hearing but only a little while afterwards, prompted by the momentum built up on the day.

Objectives

You should thus have some fixed objectives in mind prior to arriving. This is, after all, your day in court. It can be cathartic - an opportunity to divest yourself of the problem on terms acceptable to both you and the other disputants. Therefore it is too important an occasion to waste due to inadequate preparation, inability to negotiate or unwillingness to listen closely to the other side. A representative will only be of use in the process if he or she understands that the basis of the conflict has now become an object of discussion rather than a partisan contest, as the parties try to educate the mediator what needs to be done to satisfy each side.

Working with the Mediator - Tactical Considerations

The mediator wishes to get a settlement. It is not his or her function to be an advocate, or to evaluate a position or advance what is fair. He is not concerned with whether the settlement is objectively fair. Having said that he is impartial, and must be trusted not to breach confidence. You must consider the issue of mutual trust and confidence between you and your legal team and work at it to enable the mediator to do his job.

The mediator's training and technique is to get you to re-assess your expectation, position and risk, if necessary by undermining your assessment of appropriate or effective settlement levels. He is likely to see you, and probably more so your lawyer, as resistant to the appropriate settlement level, at least at the outset of the mediation and perhaps for much of the day.

As the day progresses the mediator will look for the parties' underlying joint interests, and probe for the means to bring these closer and closer until, if possible, they overlap. This he or she will do by forcing each party to clarify its position. He keeps track of each party's changing stance; he directs the parties' attention from unproductive presentations, subtly analyses their line of reasoning and encourages them to broaden their perspective; he invents or helps new lines of progress towards workable solutions; he allows for the venting of emotional tensions and outbursts, and these he deflects or absorbs so as to encourage the parties to progress towards a settlement by generating an atmosphere of problem-solving enquiry. He will then have the lawyers assist him to draw together settlement options into a coherent package.

Although initially you may regard the mediator as a quasi-judge and the process as some sort of quasi-trial, the advantages of the private session should dispel such notions. Here you are free from the stress of observation by the other side or by a judge. The mediator should promote the sense of privacy to make you feel safe, and advance the dynamics of uninterrupted private communication. This is a three way process in which you have a relationship not only with your lawyer but also with the mediator.

First, always be aware that the mediator will drive a wedge between you and your lawyer if he thinks the lawyer is acting to impede a settlement. This problem can be overcome if you or your lawyer are ready with innovative proposals, particularly those that add value to the process by solutions that are not available to a judge or arbitrator. The mediator will look for hidden agendas that reveal the parties' true interests.

One of the important ways in which the mediator adds value to the negotiating process as a recognised neutral is to deal with the situation known as reactive devaluation: this is where you are likely to place the worst interpretation on, or assume the worst intention of, an offer or statement coming from someone you regard as untrustworthy, where the same offer coming from someone seen as a friend or someone detached (i.e. the mediator) will either seem better or can at least be assessed more objectively. You should use the mediator to discuss proposals and options, and this is particularly where you need to be frank with him about the real value of your position.

Although progress is driven by the ambit and momentum of the negotiations, you must remember that it is only the mediator who knows what both sides want. His aim will be to understand the parties' true interests and consequently obtain offers that overlap so that each party will obtain a settlement with which they are happy. This may not coincide with your strict legal rights, but if you are in fact happy, do not let that concern you.

Throughout the day your team should keep an eye on the mediator to ensure he is:

- including everyone in discussions;

- listening attentively to what has been said;

- demonstrating his understanding by responding and summarising;

- being neutral, open and non-judgmental;

- being approachable, open, friendly, and even-handed;

- observing and demonstrating confidentiality at all times.

How do I deal with the mediator?

You must prepare and develop a settlement strategy, keeping the goal of mediation firmly in mind: you are there to settle, to stop the litigation costs clock running, and to stop your time being wasted by being engaged in the dispute, thus enabling you to get on with your business and your life. This means having an agenda that you may or may not want to disclose to the mediator. It may be in your interest, initially at least, to let the mediator know only part of your ambition, although generally as soon as you feel confident in trusting the mediator he or she should be told all your needs and wants.

You are more likely to succeed by being entirely cooperative towards the mediator, whether or not you agree with his approach. Promote interest-based negotiation and creative settlement options, engage in brainstorming, separate people issues from problem issues, and look for objective and independent or external criteria to justify settlement proposals; understand how to reciprocate; find ways to cross the last gap, justify splitting differences, and advance the last offer.

Here are some general suggestions borne out of experience:

- Avoid extreme opening offers and incremental concessions.

- Don't use artificial tactics which he will have been trained to see through - stonewalling, threatening, becoming angry, intimidating, ridiculing, or indeed, lying. In particular try not to lie to the mediator. Although he is not a judge and the mediation is not a court setting, it is not very becoming conduct or attractive, will embarrass your lawyer if discovered or other members of your team, is usually unproductive and potentially very damaging to the settlement dynamics if discovered by either the mediator or the other side. It will lead to an immediate loss of the trust and confidence necessary to provide the momentum towards settlement, which might be impossible to recover.

- Be courteous.

- Do not talk over the mediator or demonstrably fail to listen.

- Do not fake paying attention.

- Do not fail to disclose helpful information.

- Do not fix upon a single solution or run to the bottom line too quickly.

- Do not make allegations in bad faith as a negotiating tool, or fail to prioritise your true needs.

- Do not assume the mediator will communicate with the other side as directed by you - merely because he is given permission to carry some piece of information or even offer to the other side do not assume that he will do so, either when asked or at all.

Among your agenda items will be those matters you wish to prioritise: make sure you know what these are, and in due course, ensure the mediator is also aware of whatever is crucial. Understand the relative value to you of each issue you want to raise. Assess the realistic chances of success for each, bearing in mind that such an assessment is likely to change, and you will probably have to give way in a number of areas.

Work out how to apply your strategy according to the pace of the day. Negotiations usually start very slowly, with each side trying to justify its position to the mediator as a pre-cursor to making any offer; the tempo picks up as offers are finally exchanged and the settlement begins to crystallise, and then slows down at the end when difficult concessions have to be made - with the final arguments often being raised over relative minutiae. Applying your tactics to the pace of what is going on will enable you to assess when to offer more and when to stand firm, particularly in dealing with optimism bias, that is, the over optimistic forecast of the opposing lawyer and his client, and indeed, your own position. Know when to move, how far and in what direction.

In formulating your strategy for the day:

(i) Determine the value of your settlement position in respect of each issue in dispute. Judge what concessions can be made at little cost.

(ii) Identify new factors that might cause you to change your mind about the viability of your case e.g. new or clarified information; the capabilities of the other side now that you have seen them.

(iii) Develop a structured negotiation plan. Work out the point at which you will settle and how to get there.

(iv) Avoid basing your offer or demand on the age of the case as it is being litigated or on its current position. The dynamics of mediation mean that cases settle there much earlier than in litigation, often before statements of case and generally well before disclosure or the exchange of witness statements.

(v) Plan to offer or demand at the mediation what you eventually will or hope to settle for. There is no point in holding back and hoping for a better outcome post-mediation.

(vi) At the mediation don't see the mediator merely as a messenger, conveying offers with shuttle diplomacy. He or she will obtain information and use or re-frame it as they consider appropriate. Allow and expect him to have some leeway in developing possible outcomes.

(vii) Don't insist on monetary responses to your last offer. The mediator may get movement in principle in which each side tests offers without having to disclose, or yet disclose, a specific amount, for example 'we'll move if the other side moves'. You can test and make offers in general terms without having to disclose a specific amount.

(viii) Be candid with the mediator. Assist him to persuade the other side of the merits of your position, or how best to persuade them of it. He cannot act as a judge, but he can usefully identify and try to overcome misunderstandings and break down the problem of communication gaps leading to credibility issues, lack of trust between the parties and emotional or other grievances.

(ix) Determine whether there are, and if so identify, any facts you do not want the mediator to disclose to your opponent. But bear in mind if you have facts which will affect the outcome of the contest, not much is to be gained by concealing them if the only difference is whether you settle now or later. There may be facts you do not want to tell the other side, but which may be helpful for the mediator to know in confidence.

(x) Consider the position from the other side's perspective. How would your opposite number approach the debate?

(xi) Discuss your negotiating/settlement strategy with your lawyer or representative; tell him what you intend doing and why. Give regularly updated instructions on settlement during the course of the mediation when you are together privately.

(xii) Understand and apprehend the mediator's tactics, particularly how he will try to undermine your confidence in the strengths of your case even if he is a facilitative mediator.

A useful tool is to create a checklist for each stage of the negotiations. This will help clarify the current position and focus your thoughts on the next round:

1. Where do negotiations stand now?

2. Within what range will I settle?

3. Do I need to adjust the range to accommodate what I now know?

4. What do I need to learn from other side which will impact on that range?

5. What offers/demands can I make to get within the range?

If you are acting for a large corporation or institution you should be conscious of the possibility of tension arising among your own party, for example between the ultimate decision maker and the person responsible for the dispute occurring. This may extend to friction between your principal and your representative - remember, agents have interests of their own which are rarely perfectly aligned with their client. A mediator may need to exploit this tension if he can identify it, and you will need a defensive strategy when that occurs.

Do not worry about being seen to be co-operative. A conciliatory approach does not mean folding. Your task is to conduct a principled and structured negotiation. That will make progress more readily than your robustness. The mediator will appreciate assistance in reaching his goal, although assisting the mediator does not extend to abandoning a firm position. If you are flagging or becoming drained ask for a break, and if necessary, an adjournment.

Your tactics may in fact be dictated by express instructions from your insurers. Some claims managers now have considerable experience of mediation and feel that they can exploit the process by being tough negotiators. For example they may make offers only open for acceptance on the day of the mediation or prejudicial information might be produced which has not been seen before, or a defendant's insurer may simply refuse to increase an offer. You need to be in a position to deal with such scenarios, to protect yourself and to maintain your self-belief.

Working Towards a Settlement

Perhaps the most difficult notion to grasp is that you do not need to obtain a legal solution to the problem, even if you have been heavily engaged in litigation and even if your lawyer has urged you that is the case. It is not necessary to build the settlement around rights and liabilities, just needs and interests. Rights and liabilities are only relevant in terms of projecting the likely outcome of a trial for the purpose of applying pressure to settle. Your underlying interests may have nothing to do with rights or liabilities. If the mediator can expose these interests, practical and creative solutions may be available, at least as options. That is why lateral and creative thinking are so important to the process.

You must know your BATNA (best alternative to a negotiated agreement) and how to calculate it and improve on it if possible. So, what is the best probable outcome you could achieve in terms of an award of money plus interest, plus recoverable legal costs and disbursements. However, can you also get compensation for the value of your management time, the opportunity cost to your business, the damage to your reputation, the fragmentation of your relationship, the effect of the ongoing dispute on your health, and the stress on co-workers or your family? All of these at least should be factored into establishing your BATNA, since you and your negotiating team, and ultimately the mediator, need to know the best you think you can achieve if you cannot get a deal at the mediation.

Equally you must know the WATNA (worst alternative to a negotiated agreement) and ensure that this includes the costs of both sides and interest involved in taking a case to trial and losing. But more than this, you should anticipate the other side's equivalent position: "The more you can learn of their options the better prepared you are for negotiation. Knowing their alternatives, you can realistically estimate what you can expect from the negotiation. If they appear to overestimate their BATNA, you will want to lower their expectations. (Fisher R., and Ury W, *Getting to Yes: Negotiating an Agreement Without Giving In* Penguin 2003 p.109)

Be curious about your opponent's position. Try to find the breakthrough or 'tipping point', which will cause movement and generate a sufficient momentum to bring about the settlement. You need to achieve a deal that suits everyone, since that is the desired outcome without which you will not be able to get anything you want: there is a balance to be struck between protecting your own interests by declining to offer concessions and failing to get any advantageous agreement at all.

You also need to discover what the other side really wants. You have to be as much aware as the mediator of the difference between positions and interests, demands and needs, and claims and motivations. A trained mediation advocate will be able to help you in this.

Always be aware that ADR is concerned with the appropriateness to the client of the dispute resolution - this process is intended to meet your best needs for resolving the dispute. Contrast this with litigation, where most of the court process is designed to compensate harm with an award of money. That is a pernicious doctrine because in many cases money is only a poor substitute for the loss suffered, particularly a physical or psychological injury. (The themes in this section are developed from the investigatory work of Professor Gerald R. Williams, J Reuben Clark Law School, Brigham Young University, Utah, USA drawn from his Materials on Negotiation and Conflict Resolution for Lawyers used in the CEDR seminar *'Are You a Co-operative or Aggressive Negotiator and Does it Matter? Lawyers as Healers and Warriors*. September 1997 afterwards referred to as 'Williams'.)

Do not think that, while important, money is everything. The process of negotiation is not simply a process of bargaining where you are haggling to get nearer to your side of the middle of a monetary amount. The mediator will be looking for a way to enable you to evaluate the potential for joint gains and discover the interests and needs of *both* sides, including money but not exhaustively. Negotiation is interaction with a goal in mind.

The Negotiation Stage within Mediation

Competent and effective negotiation must be the subject of adequate preparation. For the purpose of preparing this stage of the mediation:

- You must feel ready, otherwise do not negotiate.

- You need to provide the mediator with sufficient facts to provide him with a better understanding of the true nature of the case.

- Decide what your objectives are: money, or money plus other joint interests.

- Have a clear strategy as to how you will reach your goals.

- Try to keep part of the process task orientated: make the other side work to prove their negotiating position by demonstrating where the numbers come from.

- Devise questions for the other side that can only be answered by the client, not his lawyer, to draw the opposite party directly into the process.

- Make sure you can come to settlement.

Most people are conflict avoiders - they will absorb the harm done to them in order to get on with their lives - or at least they are conflict neutral. They are pushed into conflict by a straw that breaks the camel's back. They ascribe blame to the person or entity they perceive is doing them harm, and raise a claim. They need an avenue through which to channel conflict when their claim is rejected. That avenue leads to negotiation, mediation, arbitration and trial. (Burgess, John *Mediation Skills: What the Mediator Wants from Advocates* 1 Serjeants Inn seminar February, 2005.)

Mediation is assisted or managed negotiation. But in spite of its flexibility and its advantages over an arbitral system, mediation cannot escape from the necessary party rituals embodied in negotiation.

First you must understand the difference between positional and principled negotiation. In litigation the lawyer who has to negotiate will generally engage in positional bargaining or haggling. Here each side takes up a position based on the outcome needed. The negotiator will focus on why he needs a particular outcome and what he can offer in return or demand as part of the process. He will haggle, threaten, or swap concessions and usually agree somewhere in the middle of the bargaining range. The difficulty with positional bargaining is that to improve the outcome, generally by extending the bargaining range at one end so as to accommodate a movement nearer your position than half way, subject to professional ethics, there is an incentive to misrepresent the position, or your interests, to withhold sensitive information, make threats, bluff, dig your heels in or wait unreasonably, fail to listen to the other side, make only small and low concessions, make no concession without getting a return, and, occasionally, use walking out as a tactic. This approach is likely to produce only a limited outcome, and one that might give rise to future problems if there is an ongoing relationship.

Principled bargaining is a problem solving method in which you aim for a wise outcome produced in an efficient and amicable way, by negotiating on merits not merely advancing claims. Mediators are taught to work 'hard on the problem, soft on the people', to use objective criteria, to separate the personality issues from the problem, to focus on interests and invent options for mutual gain. Mediators therefore tend to move positional bargaining into principled bargaining. The dynamic works because the mediator has no stake in the dispute - a party is therefore less likely to adopt a positional negotiating stance with the mediator and is therefore more likely to reveal his real objectives and what he is prepared to concede.

The mediator introduces the element of 'objective criteria' into the parties' understanding of their own position. He can, if asked and he agrees, give an outside view on the validity of the case or the fairness of a proposal (although this 'evaluative' model is distinctly frowned on by the UK mediation industry). He will exploit the differences between the parties' perceptions of risk. He will seek to build momentum towards a settlement by obtaining movement on a number of easy items. He may suggest non-party assistance in resolving difficult issues, by asking for further information, or provide tasks for the parties on each side to perform, such as number crunching. He will look for productive trade-offs, for example by suggesting that if the other side are willing to move on this, you should move on that.

The mediator will break up the formality or rhythm of the day if he thinks it will help. He may defer certain issues. He will certainly be a constructive force: he will emphasise positive progress and diffuse language with emotional content by channeling hostility between the parties into solving problems, (an approach which has been formalized into transformative mediation). An important role is to help parties save face in moving from previous strongly held positions.

There are particular stresses to be encountered in open negotiating sessions, particularly where you are having to cope with running information which may be completely new to you, evaluating offers, looking for potential problems, and understanding the risks you face. The following guidance should be of practical assistance:

- Do not agree if you disagree.

- Always think about the consequences before making a concession.

- Explain the story - make sure the other side understands what you are saying.

- Make sure you understand what the other side is saying.

- Establish within the specific context of the present negotiation what is important to you, and why, and also establish whether there is anything else which is important

- Do not lose any momentum - move on to the next objective once you have achieved all that you think you can achieve.

- Try to evaluate what is going on at all times - do not be confused by the negotiation dynamic.

- Be aware of the allocation of risk between the parties in any proposed solution to the dispute which is more creative than an award of money.

- Be aware of the allocation of risk between the parties should the mediation fail: at the point at which you stand, who will lose out more if one party decides to walk out?

- Look at the longer term.

- Anticipate problems.

- Don't take everything that is being said at face value. Read between the lines and try to decode messages.

It is far easier to negotiate in mediation if there are two or more issues to be resolved. If that is the case, negotiations involve integrating the interests of the parties. Where such interests may dovetail, there is genuine potential for joint gains, value can be created for both sides, and the available 'pie' can be expanded before it is divided. By having subsidiary issues which can be resolved either by making concessions or giving away assets without injury to your core ambition, you may be able to avoid inflicting needless harm on the opposing party and find it much easier getting to 'yes'. If, on the other hand, there is only a single issue being contested, there is only a limited distribution available, and aggressive negotiators tend to win. If there is no potential for joint gains it is difficult to argue for anything except to claim value for your own side and try to destroy the other's expectation or its investment in its own case. Therefore even single issue disputes should be deconstructed to look for potential mutual gains.

The Expected Momentum

For the mediator the appointment will run in a series of phases with which he is familiar: introductory, information gathering, reality testing, identifying solutions and problem solving, negotiation and bargaining, and settlement. Your approach to the dynamics of negotiation in a successful mediation tends to pass through five different kinds of common stages or steps, all well known to behavioural psychologists:

DENIAL

You will maintain you are not at fault, or it is not you who needs to change. You may enter the process having no conscious knowledge of the needs or desires of others, and no particular interest in meeting them unless they coincide with your own interests.

ACCEPTANCE

You concede that you *may* be part of the problem. This is a painful transition for you, but it important for you to understand from this position you can accept that even if you are not part of the problem you may be able to find or move towards the solution. (Williams, Gerald R. *A Lawyer's Handbook for Effective Negotiation and Settlement* 5th ed. West 1995. p.44)

SACRIFICE

This stage is concerned with realisation and letting go. First comes a realisation by you that there are two sides to the story in question, and the other side may have legitimate reasons for being so upset, or defensive, or vindictive; or worse, the possibility you might not win at a trial or those opposite not lose.

Having moved from your original position this transition involves something of a ritual mortification: you will have to sacrifice your pride, or greed, envy, arrogance, vanity, or conceit, and your belief in your own infallibility, your unwillingness to acknowledge another's point of view or needs, or to forgive another. It is at this point that you are at your most vulnerable, although any cathartic experience will also commence here. At this point you will need the genuine empathy of the mediator and the support of your lawyer, spouse, supporters or team members.

LEAP OF FAITH

Mediation is powerful because it facilitates leaps of faith in a way that litigation cannot. Even agreeing to mediation is a leap of faith since you may worry that this alone may be perceived by the other side as a sign of weakness. That said, once you see winning is no longer a foregone conclusion, and that some movement must come from you, using the mediator reduces the risk involved in such a leap of faith. The progress towards settlement starts with small mutually reciprocal steps, apology, an acknowledgement of wrong doing or wrong thinking, or concessions about the nature of your behaviour. This is answered hopefully by forgiveness, and that replied to with contrition. Once the emotion has been broken with a leap of faith, negotiations to create a practical solution can follow.

RENEWAL/RECONCILIATION

The final dynamic in the process is one of coming together, the healing of relations, or at least those positive feelings engendered by having reached a concluded agreement. Even if a fractured relationship is difficult to mend, the relief in having finalised the dispute gives a sense of renewal.

Negotiating Phases

Just as psychologists have identified well-defined stages in the mediation process, through which the disputants transcend, so researchers have observed that most negotiation develops through certain phases. At the beginning negotiators establish a working relationship and adopt respectively their initial bargaining positions. Aggressive negotiators will try to convey the impression that they are irrevocably committed to their opening position. This, the opening phase of the negotiation, is actually quite lengthy with no perceptible movement by either side.

The middle stage of a negotiation commences when some outside factor gives impetus to the process, usually some sort of time deadline. At that point the negotiators commence working seriously on the question of whether an agreement is possible. This is when alternative solutions, compromise and concession making are sought.

The final stage is the most crucial. As the deadline approaches a crisis is often reached: the negotiators often feel trapped by the choice of whether to accept the last offer or let the mediation fail, unless another alternative can be devised. As a process either agreement is reached or the parties declare an impasse. If there is a settlement the parties will work out the details of the agreement; if an impasse is declared, the parties will have to make alternative arrangements, such us furthering the claim in litigation.

(See Williams, Gerald R: *A Lawyer's Handbook for Effective Negotiation and Settlement* 5th edn West 1995.)

Opening Negotiating Positions

My firm advice is to make the opening offer, even if you simply want the mediator to know you are serious about a settlement: in negotiating psychology the first number is the most potent number in the negotiation since it must influence the second number, and potentially control the range in which the second number falls. It must be selected with great care, balancing the fear that you cannot get what you don't ask for, with being so aggressive that the other side want to leave immediately. You must consider the likely impact on the other side of adopting a maximalist position, which is where you ask for considerably more than you expect to obtain by making a very high opening demand.

Contrast this with actually opening by asking for what you feel is fair to both sides (the 'equitable position'), either by giving your anticipated bottom line straight away, or by inflating your demand by a 'reasonable' amount which you will afterwards concede. A party that opens with his true bottom line has no room for manoeuvre except by offering alternative or additional non-monetary solutions.

Whether you start with a maximalist or equitable opening, the effective mediation negotiator will explore a variety of alternative solutions to the dispute in the hope of arriving at an optimum solution which provides the greatest possible benefit and the least possible damage to both sides, often looking at something the other side haven't considered.

Both sides may safely assume that the opening position is a product of posturing, and that both sides will be willing to move in order to obtain a settlement. The suggestion that one side or the other is unalterably committed to its opening position is illusory, although it may take a significant amount of time for the illusion to be dispelled since it will have been supported by reference to the legal and factual elements of the case.

Movement

The first impediment to securing movement in the negotiations is overcoming bluff and getting the other side to enter seriously into dialogue. It is a convention among lawyers to pretend that the lawyer who first suggests settlement has the weaker case; by the same token many lawyers believe that by holding out against settlement discussions they imply that theirs will be a winning case at trial. This is particularly true of insurer defendants and defence lawyers, for whom delay is normally advantageous. Both of these beliefs have led to cases proceeding to trial only to settle hurriedly at the last moment. A waste for all, except the lawyers.

By electing to go to mediation, or having been nudged in that direction by the court, you have the benefit of the same context for negotiation, but the absence of pressure will pervade the opening part of the day unless there is strong independent motivation for the parties to start coming together. Movement comes only as the day wears on and it is apparent that there will be no point to the mediation without it: one party or the other will be asked by the mediator to put up or shut up - he will press both sides to say in terms whether they are here to obtain a settlement or not. At that point your predetermined scheme for subtly reducing your opening position should come into effect, either as the prime mover or in reply to a hint of movement from the other side. At the outset it need not be explicit or even a formulated cash offer, and can be based on principle - 'if you move, so will we'. Eventually the degrees of movement will crystallise into firm offers which usually also conform to a recognised pattern. This involves initially small movement followed by fairly large-scale movement, and then finally, very small-scale movement as you tentatively approach settlement. Invariably the last steps are the hardest.

Crisis and Deadlock

The point of crisis comes with the arrival of a deadline, or the apparent reaching of a limit to authority, and these can both give rise to intense psychological pressure imposed by a strong opponent and the mediator, who will each try to use it. You may be faced with what you perceive to be the final offer from the other side; or the mediator may be relying upon a 'locked-door' syndrome to achieve a breakthrough. The pressure comes with the realisation by you and your party that should the last offer be refused the mediation will fail, and further litigation costs will be expended, and the trial perceived as inevitable; alternatively if the last offer is accepted you will never know if you could have achieved more or paid less.

The way to break this psychological pressure is to remember that you are in fact not caught in a yes/no situation. You always have three choices: (i) to accept your opponent's last offer, (ii) to reject your opponent's last offer, walk away and go to trial, or (iii) to come up with a new proposal. It is the third choice that is often the key to success. This third option prevents unnecessary deadlock, keeps the negotiation alive and puts pressure on your opponent to accept your revised offer. The closer you are to the deadline, the more seriously your opponent must consider your offer. Therefore always be in a position to modify your last offer as the best way to save face at the moment of deadlock, keep the process going and deflect the pressure of the crisis point to the other side.

Remember that the deadline may not be uniform and for reasons unknown to you the other side may have an entirely different time limit of their own. Deadlines can relate to the litigation, for example the imminence of the trial, the next case management conference or court direction, after the lifting of any automatic stay pending dispute resolution, or they can be fact related, for example the next delivery or payment due, the application of pressure from the bank on your credit, the next tranche of legal fees due, or pressure coming from other sources.

The pre-arranged end of the mediation session is also a deadline that creates strong psychological pressure, although this is usually artificial since, if the parties wish to continue and the mediator considers it worthwhile, either the mediation or bi-partisan negotiations can continue by agreement. If you or your lawyer have a particular personal deadline - catching the last train, or flying out - it is unwise to reveal this as your opponent may use such a difficulty as a pressure point, even if he is the most cooperative of negotiators.

Dealing With Obnoxious Opponents

What do you do when faced with an opponent who is irritating, rigid, hostile, arrogant, quarrelsome and egotistical? How do you negotiate with such a person? The key is self-control. You must not give way to your basic impulse to fight fire with fire - if you lose your own patience and goodwill the negotiations will be over before they start and your side will leave the mediation with a strong sense of wasted time and costs, which you may blame on the process itself. The fighting fire with fire approach will almost certainly lead to deadlock and failure.

Your aim is to outwit such negotiators by calling their bluff, putting maximum pressure on them to change their tactics and deal with you on a realistic and rational level. To do so you need to exercise enormous restraint to prevail successfully against an irritating opponent. Keep your temper. Don't quarrel. Give him a soft answer (at the risk of maddening him).

Use the mediator to help you adopt a position that you will not negotiate with this person so long as the irritating tactics continue: do not initiate negotiations while they do, and do not accede to your opponent's attempts to negotiate. Keep occasional or even frequent contact to educate him about the case, refer him to key facts and documents, or indicate key developments on your side. The mediator will reframe your communications to make them non-threatening and invite cooperation. Direct the mediator to express empathy and openly promise that you will commence your negotiation when the time is right. But all the time refuse to negotiate so long as the irritating tactics continue. Indicate your preparedness for the litigation to go on.

(For this argument developed see: Williams *Solving Particular Problems In Legal Negotiation* op.cit. pp57-61.)

Dealing With Overly Aggressive Opponents

When facing an effective aggressive opponent it is well to understand four basic defensive principles:

   (i) Know you are under attack.

  (ii) Know what kind of attack you're facing. Learn to judge and recognise your opponent's weapons, his strength and his level of skill.

 (iii) Know how to make your defence fit the attack - the response must match each aggressive move, it must be an appropriate response and at an appropriate level of intensity - proportionate and sufficient to secure your aim.

 (iv) Know how to follow through - you must be able to carry out your response once you have chosen it. Be prepared to feel and work through a certain amount of guilt, since healthy people don't enjoy causing other people pain even when it is well and thoroughly deserved.

When attempting to defuse the potency of an aggressive opponent, as a cooperative negotiator you will need to:

- Deal more effectively with the facts: accept the burden of demonstrating the credibility of your own facts. Prove you have something worth paying for.

- Recognise that your aggressive opponent will skilfully seek to discredit your facts. He and his client will have set their expectations by how far you are willing to let them go. Stay with your facts until your opponent recognises that there are strong points in your case and understands what they are.

- Present facts serially, not all together. Look for the reaction of your opponent on an item-by-item basis and decide what to do by reading the reaction.

- Present your facts in their strategically most favourable light.

- Recognise that parties inevitably have a different view of the facts. Do not try to persuade your opponent to adopt your view of the facts, rather to take your view of them into account.

- Express willingness to change your view if he can demonstrate his position convincingly.

- Repeat the facts as often as they are challenged. Often the aggressive negotiator's strategy is to ignore or refute your facts. The solution is to show that your facts can sustain his attack.

- Adopt opening positions favourable to you but clearly communicate that the position is temporary since the parties' interests and needs are not yet fully known, that some facts require more careful consideration, and that you invite and seek a creative solution for joint gains.

- Make few unilateral concessions, and never make a unilateral concession on the merits.

- Make only concessions that do not hurt your position. Withhold any major concessions until a suitable package can be put together - make it at least a two-stage process. In order to preserve the negotiating climate you can acknowledge the other sides' interests and needs, and indicate that concessions will be made, but explain with good reasons why they are not available at present.

- Respond immediately and unambiguously to aggressive moves. Avoid mirroring aggressive behaviour but use a counter move: require an explanation, or a reference to the facts; cushion your response with empathy; express a recognition that a different point of view might be valid; admit your source of information may be wrong; use the need for consultation and instructions as a buffer, but never flatly refuse - give reasons, and consistently decline to make unwise or premature concessions; elaborate factors which weigh against granting requests, keep your client's options open, leave room to manoeuvre, and, like a proverbial boy scout, be prepared and look prepared.

- When dealing with this kind of an opponent refuse to 'play the same game.' Disarm him by asking 'why' frequently - seek explanations for demands being made - and have him identify what are the interests sought to be met by the demands he is making. Look for objective criteria. And try to shame him - question his sense of fairness and whether he really wants a settlement.

Dealing With Opposing Lawyers

Most lawyers will deal with you courteously and in a business-like manner if they see you are unrepresented. Their code of professional conduct requires them to do so, and it is in their interest and that of their client to act in keeping with the aim of the enterprise in the presence of the mediator. Do not let the conduct of opposing lawyers anger, upset or distract you. Their role is to advance your opponent's case, and they want to jockey their client into a position of strength for the negotiation phase. Keep your eyes on the ultimate objective of the process. It is to achieve a settlement. Throughout the mediation use these guiding principles:

- Clearly say what you really mean.

- Learn what your opponent really means.

- Do not assume either party (including your own principle where appropriate) does not have ulterior motives for taking part in the mediation, the most obvious being to discover information.

- Do not assume any inequality of power can be rectified because the mediator is present.

- Do not assume the other side will accept either information given or a proposal when made.

- Do not assume everything said at the mediation will in fact remain confidential - a party might use it indirectly, and parties may breach or waive confidentiality.

- Once you have reached a settlement do not indicate in any way that you feel you have gotten the better of your opponent: convey only that it was a good deal for both parties.

- Never suggest that you might have made more concessions or accepted a lower offer.

Dealing With Your Own Feelings

As time progresses during the day you will undoubtedly have to deal with situations that make you feel uncomfortable on a personal level. This is perfectly normal, particularly when you have started from a bullish position as a result of advice previously given to you about the strength of your case. Under reality testing by the mediator, or having heard the other side's lawyer in open session, your perceptions may well change. Strategies that help include:

- Finding ways to save face when you retreat from a previously held position or advice.

- Establishing the reason for a change in your negotiating position: you need to justify it to yourself as well as the mediator.

- Taking 'time out' to reflect.

The Impact of Relations with your Legal Team

You should anticipate that on some occasions - fortunately these are becoming increasingly rare as lawyers become educated as mediation advocates - getting to settlement may require the mediator to drive a wedge between you and your lawyers, at least to the extent of undermining the advice you are being given, which the mediator may feel is acting as a brake on the momentum. This may cause tension between you and your representative which could leave you confused, nervous, bewildered, or angry. The danger is you may be led to unwise decisions.

This problem arises because to an extent your lawyer may feel you need to be protected from the mediator as well as the other side, particularly if he or she takes a bullish view of the merits of your case. You must then ensure the lawyer fully understands your wider interests, and try to judge objectively whether the mediator is right - are you better off with your lawyer taking more of a back seat role or is the mediator going for broke because that is his personal agenda? There may come a point at which you have to ask a pro-active lawyer to let you deal directly with the mediator. This is a difficult call because first, you need the confidence to do this, and second, it deprives the lawyer of the opportunity to demonstrate how he is earning his fee.

Alternatively the situation may develop where your lawyer may consider that the other side or the mediator is being reasonable and you are actually being recalcitrant and irrational, and he is unable to make you see what is by any standards a good deal, and one unlikely to be achieved as the outcome of litigation. It is then that he will use the mediator as a foil to prevent the likely conflict between your views and his instructions.

Neither of these scenarios are uncommon, and the mediator will be aware of these dynamics. There is no reason why you should not be alert to them also.

Consider that part of the process, indeed part of the ritual, is that mediation will help the parties learn more about themselves and each other. The best way to settlement is if both parties have a change of heart - the mediator will be aiming for compromise plus reconciliation. Otherwise if parties maintain an 'all or nothing' approach they will head irrevocably towards trial.

Using Tit-For-Tat as a Model Negotiating Strategy

There is a useful method for creating a balance between cooperative and aggressive negotiation, devised for use in game theory and usually referred to as the Anatole Rappaport model of 'the Prisoner's Dilemma' (See Allman, William F *Nice Guys Finish First* Science (1984) vol 5 no 8 p25-31; Axelrod, Robert *The Evolution of Cooperation* Basic Books 1984.)

It is the simple but effective strategy known as tit-for-tat, and it is this: always begin cooperatively then respond tit-for-tat to each cooperative or aggressive move by the other side.

As a tactical device it has six qualities that make it useful when negotiating in mediations:

1. It begins cooperatively, although cooperation is based on both anticipation of and the fact that cooperation will be mutual.

2. It retaliates perfectly in the sense that the response will be immediate, unambiguous, and appropriate - the cooperative negotiator will be vigilant of attack and will react, making it clear he is acting responsively to unacceptable aggression from the other side.

3. It is perfectly trustworthy - the negotiator never moves aggressively unless he is attacked.

4. It forgives perfectly - the response is immediate, unambiguous, and appropriate.

5. It is not greedy - the response doesn't object to gains made by other side because they should be mutual.

6. It is perfectly patient: as a device it doesn't try to shortcut the negotiation process - it follows the ritual of negotiation.

Useful as tit-for-tat is in negotiation it does have one flaw of which to be wary: if one side mis-reads the other by interpreting a non-aggressive move as an attack, the misreading side will retaliate. The innocent side will respond in kind with both continuing to believe the other side started it. Such a situation can only be broken by a leap of faith by a cooperative negotiator, or by tracing the problem back to its source.

What is the impact of confidentiality?

One of the clearest views we have of the creeping juridification of mediation by the courts is the examination of privilege and confidentiality attaching to the mediation process, and, in doing so, consideration of the future compellability of the mediator. Mediator trainers and mediation service providers have long proceeded on the basis that the mediator is not compellable at trial as a witness of the contents of a previous mediation of the dispute, whether the outcome was a settlement or otherwise. This sense of security for mediators is borne out of the contractual protection usually given by the parties in the mediation agreement.

For the industry, the very essence of mediation depends upon the participants in the process being confident they can be as frank at all times and open with each other and the mediator as they would wish without fear that anything they said, or any document they produced solely for the purposes of the mediation, or any concession they may choose to make in the course of exploring a settlement, might subsequently be admitted into evidence in later court proceedings.

In England and Wales the courts have now intervened to consider this aspect of mediation on a number of recent occasions. Lord Dyson said in the *Halsey* case

> *"We make it clear that it was common ground at the outset (and we accept) that parties are entitled in an ADR to adopt whatever position they wish, and if as a result the dispute is not settled, that is not a matter for the court.... if the integrity and confidentiality of the mediation process is to be respected, the court should*

not know, and therefore should not investigate, why the process did not result in agreement."

The relevant signed mediation agreement will provide expressly for confidentiality as to the content of the mediation. Sometimes this will extend to the existence of the mediation, and/or its outcome.

As at the time of writing, the law in England and Wales appears to be this

1. Confidentiality: mediation proceedings are confidential both as between the parties and as between the parties and the mediator. As a result even if the parties agree that matters can be referred to outside the mediation, the mediator can enforce the confidentiality provision. The court will generally uphold that confidentiality but where it is necessary in the interests of justice for evidence to be given of confidential matters, the Courts will order or permit that evidence to be given or produced.

2. Without Prejudice Privilege: The proceedings are covered. This is a privilege which exists between the parties, who can waive it. It is not a privilege of the mediator.

3. Other Privileges: If another privilege attached to documents which are produced by a party and shown to a mediator, that party retains that privilege and it is not waived by disclosure to the mediator or by waiver of the without prejudice privilege.

For the purpose of this book you should assume mediation agreements will continue to specify that the mediation proceedings are conducted on a "without prejudice" basis; should continue to make it clear that what is said during mediation proceedings will be confidential, in which case you will be bound by that; and should not restrict the circumstances in which a mediator cannot be compelled to give evidence in court.

SETTLEMENT

What if I settle?

It is essential that the parties secure a concluded agreement that is workable, comprehensive, (both as to the dispute and any wider issues which have been introduced,) and enforceable. If you are represented, it is vital that you get your advocate to ensure the form of the agreement is correct and enforceable. This settlement agreement will be a document that replaces the dispute, and is in law a contract between yourself and the other side. The terms must be certain, specific, effective, practical and complete, in particular dealing with who is to do what, when, and with what precise consequences. A provision will usually need to be inserted detailing what to do if one side or the other fails to adhere to the agreement or if it proves to be unworkable.

If you are unrepresented the mediator may assist the parties in drafting brief heads of terms, that is a very broad outline of what has been agreed, which you will be asked to sign on the day, and then suggest you and your opponent instruct a lawyer jointly to have the agreement drawn up and ratified.

It is as well to take a draft containing the likely heads of agreement with you and, if litigation is running, a general form of Tomlin order (see Appendix 5). If the compromise contains terms found in a recognised standard form or precedent, do not forget to bring it with you. Otherwise you will be forced to locate it, probably at a highly inconvenient time for doing so.

As you near settlement you should begin to draft the proposed agreement in your caucus room. Your lawyer will discuss with you the contents as early as possible, since you can formulate the structure as the mediation progresses. This will help focus on the details and will place the client's personal agenda in context. (See York, Stephen D, *Preparing Your Client for Mediation* Resolutions issue 17 Summer 1997.) At this point - prior to the actual agreement - you must be clear about the practicalities of its implementation.

The agreement needs to strike a balance between too little, and too much detail. Do not be overly pedantic. Remember it is likely to be either quite late or very late, at the end of a long day. You may wish to keep the mediator informed of progress in drafting the agreement, and certainly where any problems arise.

While the document is being settled you should be aware precisely who should be the signatory. Do not assume that you are signing it yourself, since your lawyer may do so; if you are appearing for a company or institution do not do so without seeking express authority, irrespective of the fact that you are likely to have sufficient implied authority as a matter of law.

You may wish to discuss the introduction of certain standard clauses irrespective of the nature of the settlement. These should deal with:

- confidentiality;

- any relevant choice of law or jurisdiction;

- the entire agreement between the parties;

- a default mechanism to deal with future disputes;

- whether, if there is a breach of this agreement, the original cause of action should be reinstated.

The settlement-specific clauses need to be certain as to:

- payment: who pays, to whom is payment made, and how much;

- the form in which payment is to be made;

- whether payment is to be immediate or in stages;

- the mechanism for default of payment;

- the provision of interest;

- the costs of the litigation;

- the costs of the mediation;

- any public statements;

- the discontinuance or withdrawal of proceedings;

- any special clauses dealing with enforceability;

- who is the signatory, his status or authority.

Those occasions when the parties can do no more than agree outline heads of agreement should be avoided wherever possible. Saving an hour at the end of the mediation by agreeing outline heads of agreement exposes the parties to the risk of further disputes in which the argument shifts from its original subject matter to contesting what has been agreed. It is essential that the intention of the parties is made plain, and there is at least sufficient detail to ensure that an impartial reader would have a clear idea of precisely what has been agreed. If there is no time to put in the complexity of the mechanics of the transaction, or, for example, the tax implications have not been advised upon or worked out, at least draw a distinction between the agreement itself and the mechanics for performing it.

What if I don't settle?

The mediation agreement should state what happens if the parties do not reach agreement. This is usually bound up with how the mediation can end. The mediator will usually reserve the right to call the process to a conclusion if he or she sees no realistic prospect of settlement. Alternatively the time set aside for the mediation may run out, and the parties are simply left to decide whether to adjourn or finish the process.

Mediators will generally want to assist the parties by making themselves available to continue the process of managed negotiation, either informally or by telephone, or by reconstituting at some point in the future. It is therefore important that the parties are clear about any ongoing status or afterlife of the mediation, since the mediation agreement will have confidentiality provisions which affect and may govern subsequent negotiations. Under those circumstances a clear definition of the duration of the mediation and the agreement should be known to all parties and to the mediator.

If the case proceeds to litigation it often occurs that parties will try to protect their position on costs by making an open, closed, *Calderbank*,or Part 36 offer in the proceedings which is based, at least in part, on their last position in the mediation.

TIME-LIMITED MEDIATIONS

In a sense all mediations are governed by limits on time. However many litigants and their advocates may first be introduced to mediation by being asked to participate in court-annexed schemes in circumstances where the parties have not agreed to mediate beforehand. These include the Small Claims service which generally operates by telephone, but which may be outsourced to providers offering fixed three-hour mediations.

It is possible for parties to agree that a mediation should be limited in time to three or four hours, or a half-day without using a court-annexed scheme. This may be intended as a cost-saving device because there is only a single or narrow issue to be negotiated, or the parties mistakenly assume that if agreement cannot be reached in that time, it is unlikely to be reached at all.

In either case how are you to deal with the curtailment or concentration of a process, which seemingly requires the time to pass through certain phases, including time for detailed negotiations? The answer depends to an extent on the approach of the mediator. Some will try to run the mediation in precisely the same way as if there were no time constraints. If that happens the mediator will try to compress the same events and process into shorter lengths of time, hoping to arrive at a satisfactory result.

However more experienced and more confident mediators will probably jettison less important parts of the procedure and concentrate on the more important ones. For example he may either get rid of or limit the opening plenary session. In addition it may be that a guillotine is put on private caucusing. Certainly the preliminary posturing by both sides will be reduced, and offers expected far sooner than in a full day mediation. In other words the mediator will adopt a more focused approach to the management of the process and will discourage exhaustive discussion of the issues.

As you might expect, time limited mediations have a higher failure rate, particularly where the court has bounced an otherwise unwilling participant into trying them. However, in the hands of an experienced mediator, who is capable of successful time management, this process offers real value for money, in that there are no venue costs and none relating to the administration of a mediation service provider. In addition both court-annexed schemes and practising time-limited mediators will charge fees that are fixed.

As in all mediations the key to success is in the amount of pre-mediation preparation that can be completed. The fact that time is limited does not mean that you can avoid doing the necessary preparation. Quite the contrary is true. Before you attend you should have a thorough knowledge of the strengths and weaknesses of your own case, including arguments on liability and quantum, interest and causation; you need to know much the same about the case of your opponent; you need detailed information on the costs position of both sides, both historic and projected. Thus you will want to know the costs to date, the likely time to trial, and the likely duration and costs of the trial.

There will be an extremely limited bundle of core documents made available to the mediator, often consisting of nothing more than the statements of case. If there is time in advance the mediator may contact you beforehand, but again, that is unlikely. Under court-annexed schemes he will be paid extremely low rates. Fixed price fees in the private sector also allow for very little pre-mediation reading in by the mediator.

Before arriving you should be well aware of what to bring and how you are going to proceed. Your tactics will be far less sophisticated. But in each phase of the mediation the other side has to be persuaded that there is something in it for them.

Make a list of objective criteria: establish what it is you want by 7 p.m. (or 2 p.m.) that you haven't got now. Then consider the process: how to get what you want in a way that is most effective. Take a view of the most efficient use of your time, and that of any other attendees. Put short time fragments into a framework. Know what high figure and what low figure to request when the mediator asks for your position. That will be your negotiation range. Be able to explain to the mediator why there is a gap between the figures. Know how much it will cost to fight the gap, particularly whether the gap is less than the cost of going to trial. That may be the determinative factor in accepting the last offer or walking away.

If there are insurers ask them to provide their risk cost analysis. The mediator may well ask for this. He will certainly ask the defendants what sort of a settlement they are looking for, and hope to move it into the claimant's negotiating range.

Remember that short as it is, it is still your day in court. Help negotiate a settlement with which you can be comfortable at the end of the session. Do not allow yourself to be bullied into an agreement simply because of the shortage of time. Ensure that you understand and are happy, albeit reluctantly, with any offer by the other side, which you believe cannot be improved upon.

COSTS ISSUES

Can I recover the costs of the mediation?

Can I recover other costs?

What about legal costs or other expenses?

A number of costs issues arise in the context of mediation, namely

- Mediation Costs

- Litigation Costs and ADR

- The Recoverability of Costs

- Mediation Costs and Conditional Fee Arrangements (CFAs)

Mediation Costs

Mediation does not operate in a vacuum. As a process it is entirely contractual, and hopefully, it succeeds in producing a further enforceable contract which settles the dispute between the parties. That being so it is for the parties to contract between themselves who will be responsible for the costs of the mediation. These include the costs of the mediator, any separate charge by a service provider for administration or for room hire and refreshments, and the costs of party representatives and experts or other professional participants, for example accountants.

Most standard form mediation agreements provide for the costs of the mediation to be met by the parties equally, and usually provide for at least some payment in advance. There is nothing to prevent parties negotiating something different, and this occasionally happens where there is substantial inequality of arms, or a party is trying to induce the other side to come to mediation at all. During the course of the mediation a party may make it a term of the settlement that the agreement be varied to the extent that the mediation costs are provided for.

The costs of the mediation should properly be defined in the mediation agreement to avoid confusion. It may be the case that parties will return their own contribution to the cost of the mediator and the room hire, but where the dispute proceeds to litigation afterwards, they may try to recover their legal costs of the mediation as costs in the litigation.

Litigation Costs and ADR

When deciding whether to mediate, the issue of costs, particularly what costs you are likely to recover, is usually a crucial consideration. Before considering this issue, it is important to remember that mediations are not cheap per se: they are an attractive alternative to litigation, which either proceeds to trial or at least has a substantial amount of costs expended upon it in the stages leading up to trial.

However the assertion by the mediation industry that mediation presents substantial cost savings by comparison with full-scale litigation is based on the assumption that the mediation will succeed. Should the mediation fail, or merely create a momentum towards settlement but which requires further steps to be taken in the litigation, the costs of the mediation will have to be aggregated with the litigation costs. If that occurs the costs of a mediation without settlement may be significant.

There are a number of reasons why mediations can be costly. These might include the following:

- Over the last few years the mediation process has been getting far more sophisticated in the hands of the lawyer representatives. Thus representatives approach (and should approach) the preparation for a mediation in the same way as a preparation for a trial, albeit with different procedures and using different advocacy techniques; they must allot adequate preparation time, including a pre-mediation conference with the client as necessary to identify the true negotiating parameters.

- Fees must take into account pre-appointment preparation, to include settling a case summary for the mediator and possibly a reply to that of the other side, and having personal communications with the mediator in advance of the appointment.

- In assessing fees for the mediation day itself the litigator will be conscious of the fact that even mediations starting early in the morning may not conclude until well into the evening. It may be necessary to have a fee for the day with an additional hourly rate for after-court hours, alternatively a fee for a day and a half.

- In addition it will have to be decided whether expert evidence will be necessary for the mediation, and if so the form it should take, and the directions if any, for pre-appointment exchange of reports or summaries. This may extend to property, tax or other accountancy advice on the nature and operation of the proposed settlement

- Witness statements or at least summaries may be necessary.

- As with arbitration, the parties are directly contributing to the costs of the mediator and the venue.

- There may be ancillary costs (hidden or open) which are payable to the mediation service provider (e.g. cost of catering, photocopying etc). An MSP is likely to build in a profit element into its administration fee.

On the other hand, mediations can be cheaper than litigation, and the flexibility of the mediation process is a reason why costs savings can be achieved. For example:

- The speed of the process restricts the amount of chargeable time likely to be incurred.

- The absence of formal structure means that the parties are free to choose the procedure, including the degree of formality or otherwise. They will certainly wish to dispense with matters that can result in a significant cost saving.

- There is no formality about Part 20 claims or third or other additional parties. The procedure is thus far less expensive than a multi-party claim in litigation.

- The mediation is not a trial or tribunal: since the process is non-adjudicatory no findings need be made. Evidence, disclosure and documentation are substantially reduced and may be dispensed with altogether.

- There are no costs associated with the delivery of a judgment or consideration of an appeal.

- Moreover, the litigation may (and under CPR case management invariably will) be suspended by agreement during the mediation process to prevent further litigation costs accruing outside the mediation.

The Recoverability of Costs

Any analysis of what costs might be recoverable has to take into account all the situations in which a client might have incurred costs, including the costs of the mediation and of the litigation.

Costs of the Mediation in the Litigation

Parties have the freedom to choose how costs flow in mediation. The conventional principle in litigation that the loser pays the winner's costs is often alien to a resolution process whose fundamental approach is that both parties feel that they have achieved a benefit from participation. As has been suggested above, ordinarily each party will pay an equal share of the costs of the mediation to the service provider in advance, unless agreed otherwise, and a clause acknowledging liability for a share of the mediation costs will be contained in the mediation agreement. This avoids the cost of the mediation becoming an issue within the mediation. Parties can make it an issue if they wish but this will be an extra and unnecessary sticking point, which may impede settlement. Thus, unless otherwise agreed, parties to a mediation should expect to pay in advance for half the costs of the mediator, the room hire and any service fee to the mediation service provider, and pay their own costs of legal representation.

Litigation Costs in the Mediation

Liability for litigation costs forms part of the claim being mediated. It is an issue that parties' representatives *must* confront before the mediation. Thus parties to a mediation are not properly prepared unless they attend knowing:

- The amount of costs they have incurred to date (including the costs of the mediation) - this needs to be as specific as possible.

- A good estimate of the likely costs that will be incurred to the end of the trial if necessary.

- A reasonable estimate of the recoverable/irrecoverable element of their total costs on detailed assessment (on the standard and indemnity bases of assessment).

In addition, either before, or during, the mediation each party ought to obtain from any other party details of that other party's costs, including an estimate of their costs to date, of their likely future costs, and of the recoverable/irrecoverable element of their total bill.

Mediation Costs in the Litigation

Should the mediation fail or the litigation not be settled until after the mediation process has concluded, the legal costs of the mediation will usually be claimed by the successful party as part of his litigation costs. This remains something of a grey area, particularly where the mediation is not court-directed. However two frequently deployed arguments, are as follows:

- The mediation agreement is a complete collateral contract which stands outside the litigation and accordingly self-regulates the costs. To the extent that the mediation agreement does not specify the parties' liability for costs, they are borne by the party incurring them. If this argument succeeds, then the costs provided for within the agreement e.g. that each party pay a specified proportion of the costs of the mediator, the room hire and any service fee to the mediation service provider would be provided for but that all other costs would be irrecoverable.

- The mediation has narrowed down the issues in dispute which should be reflected in an appropriate costs order having regard to any direction of the court in the exercise of its discretion to award costs.

Ordinarily the court cannot open up what occurred within the mediation for the purpose of exercising its discretion as to costs in the litigation.

Mediation Costs and Public Funding

The Legal Services Commission ("LSC") favours the use of mediation to reduce publicly funded litigation. The Court of Appeal has said in the strongest terms that publicly funded claims must be mediated where possible. Public funding for mediation representation appears to have been formalised for family work (outside MIAMs) in the LSC Funding Code and was strongly endorsed by a National Audit Office Report on Legal Aid and Mediation for People Involved in Family Breakdown (26 February 2007). In principle there seems to be no reason why litigators acting for a party having the benefit of an unqualified public funding certificate should not recover their fees in a mediation. However, the availability of public funding in nearly all areas of civil litigation and substantial areas of family disputes has now all but dried up.

Mediation Costs and Litigation Funding

The legal costs which you incur for mediation will not be regarded by your lawyers as any different to the costs of litigating the same dispute, even though they may be incurred as a self-contained part of it. Your means of funding may therefore become an important consideration in terms of (i) overall recoverability and (ii) calculating your BATNA and WATNA (ii) negotiation tactics that might be employed by you or by the other side during the course of the mediation.

The impact of the Jackson reforms to civil litigation which have variously come into being after 1 April 2013 will have had an impact on the recoverability of costs consequential to their being funded by a Conditional Fee Agreements ("CFA"), a Damages

Based Agreement ("DBA"), Qualified One Way Costs Shifting ("QOCS") or a Public Funding Certificate (formerly 'Legal Aid'). The precise detail of these and your particular arrangements are outside the scope of this book.

At its simplest a conditional fee agreement ("CFA") allows a solicitor to act for a client on the basis that he will not charge his client, or not charge him as much, if an agreed result is not achieved. However a CFA is only enforceable if it complies with the various statutory requirements imposed by legislation (see generally sections 58 and 58A Courts and Legal Services Act 1990 as amended). Any agreement failing to comply with such requirements will usually be unenforceable with the result that the successful party's solicitor will not be able to recover his costs. The more recently introduced DBA represents the first time in more than 600 year of English legal history when the solicitor's fee can be taken from up to 25% of the damages recovered; and the QOCS operates to enable a winning personal injury or clinical negligence claimant to recover costs against a defendant, but suspends the operation of (i.e. enforcement) an order for costs made in favour of a winning defendant in such cases. A Public Funding Certificate may very well specify an amount that has to be repaid by a successful litigant.

I have already suggested that litigation costs are part of the claim being mediated and that as part of the mediation preparation the parties' representatives ought to obtain detailed information about their own and each other's litigation costs. However where there is a CFA/PFC, further work may need to be carried out as follows:

A funding notice should have been given to the other side to render the costs incurred under it to be recoverable

Where the settlement provides for payment of one inclusive sum representing damages and the funded party's costs, the funded representative and his client have to be clear how much each is going to recover.

It is suggested that such costs-inclusive offers have the potential to create considerable friction between client and representative, particularly where it has been deliberately calculated to do so by the other side.

The funded representative should anticipate the problem and work out a solution with the client in advance of the mediation. Otherwise the mediator may find himself having to assist in negotiations between the solicitor and his own client.

APPENDICES

1. Glossary of Common Mediation Terms

A

Adjudication A broad term describing a category of dispute resolution processes in which a third party neutral makes some form of decision on the outcome of the case. In England and Wales this specifically applies to construction disputes under the Housing Grants, Construction and Regeneration Act 1996 and successor statutory schemes where summary interim binding decisions on contractual disputes are made without following the procedures of litigation or arbitration.

ADR (Alternative Dispute Resolution) A range of procedures for the resolution of disputes that serve as alternatives to litigation through the courts. Commonly they involve the assistance of a neutral and impartial third party, either acting in a binding or non-binding arbitral capacity, or in a mediative or conciliatory capacity assisting the parties to their own solution. For some commentators, the encroaching proximity of court rules has meant a change in the use of the acronym to Amicable Dispute Resolution (ICC Rules), Appropriate Dispute Resolution (wide usage) or Accelerated Dispute Resolution (attributed to Grahame Aldous QC).

Arbitration A traditional and long-used private dispute process in which the parties agree to be bound by the decision of a neutral third party, the arbitrator, whose award is usually registrable and legally enforceable as a court judgment. Often structured to meet the needs of certain commercial bodies and industries, e.g. international trade, shipping and freight haulage, it has less formal procedures, with party participation in what these should be, abbreviated presentations and the undivided attention of the neutral(s). The arbitrator rules on discovery requests and disputes. The process can be binding or non-binding.

Assistant Mediator (Mediation Observer)   A newly trained mediator attending a mediation session to gain experience of the process and act as a companion to the lead mediator. The specific role of the Assistant is determined by the lead mediator but often includes note-taking, observing, drafting, co-mediating and running messages.

B

BATNA (Best Alternative To A Negotiated Agreement) A measure developed by Roger Fisher and William Ury of the Harvard Negotiation Project which enables negotiating parties to evaluate their options. The BATNA is the best result that a party could hope for if it called off the negotiations. Parties are advised to know their BATNA in some detail before attending mediation, to understand the risk analysis of failing to obtain a settlement agreement. The BATNA should not be confined to the value of or risk in a legal claim and its costs, but should extend to valuing lost opportunity or lost business, damage to reputation, and anything else of importance.

C

Caucus Private meetings which take place between the mediator and a single party to a dispute or their professional advisers. These are confidential sessions where nothing discussed can be conveyed to the opposing party without the express permission of the originator. Caucus meetings are often used to examine the important issues and needs of each party, encourage openness about weaknesses as well as strengths and discuss options for settlement.

Civil/Commercial mediation   The type of mediation commonly used in commercial disputes, for example, where two companies or other commercial/statutory bodies may be in dispute with one another. In the UK it generally is a facilitative process, where the mediator is engaged with the parties for a single day and uses both joint ('plenary') and private ('caucus')meetings between the parties to enable the mediator to gather information, reality test, manage negotiations and oversee settlement. By contrast other forms of mediation may not admit caucus meetings, or be spread out over a few weeks.

Claimant, complainant A term used for a person/institution who advances a cause of action or expresses a problem.

Co-mediation A process using two or more mediators in the same mediation. Co-mediation enables the mediators to work as a team to identify the disputed issues, develop options, consider alternatives and endeavour to reach an agreement. They generally adopt a facilitative approach where the mediator has no advisory or determinative role on the content of the dispute or the outcome of its resolution, but may advise on or determine the process of mediation whereby resolution is attempted.

Combined or hybrid dispute resolution processes are those in which the neutral plays multiple roles. For example, in conciliation and in conferencing, the dispute resolution practitioner may facilitate discussions, as well as provide advice on the merits of the dispute. In hybrid processes, such as med-arb, the practitioner first uses one process (mediation – usually facilitative but then, potentially, evaluative) and then a different one (arbitration).

Community mediation Mediation applied to deal with conflict between individuals and/or groups in the community, or to deal with group or community-based issues.

Community Mediation Service A mediation service provided is by a non-government or community organisation.

Community mediator A mediator chosen from a panel representative of the community in general.

Conciliation A dispute resolution process where the neutral third party takes an active role in a case by offering non-binding opinions or puts forward suggested terms of settlement. The term is used in mediation and distinguished by the advice or expression of opinion by the conciliator, rather than the mediator who may not offer an opinion. There is no international consistency over which process, mediation or conciliation, is the more activist and mediation is increasingly being adopted as the generic term for third-party facilitation in commercial disputes. The conciliator may make suggestions for terms of settlement, give expert advice on likely settlement terms, and have an advisory role on the content of the dispute or the outcome of its resolution, but not a determinative role.

Conferencing a general term, which refers to meetings in which the parties and/or their advocates and/or third parties discuss issues in dispute. It may also refer to the wider aspect of mediation in which a number of parties/stakeholders are involved, including supporters of others at the meeting and/or other individuals and relevant organisations to address issues and provide support (services) to uphold any agreement reached. Examples of agencies that may be involved in conferencing include the police, social services, and campaign groups, and those affected by settlement proposals.

Confidentiality The degree to which information given in the mediation cannot be passed on to others outside the process, with enforcement or protection given by operation of law.

Conflict Resolution The ending of conflict between parties. A process facilitated by communication, new understanding and sometimes formal agreement being reached.

Consensus building A process in which parties to a dispute, with the assistance of a facilitator, identify the facts and stakeholders, settle on the issues for discussion and consider options. This allows parties to build rapport through discussions that assist in developing better communication, relationships and agreed understanding of the issues.

Counselling A wide range of processes designed to assist people to solve personal and interpersonal issues and problems. Counselling has a specific meaning under the Family Law Act, where it is included as a Primary Dispute Resolution process (see PDR). Clients are individuals or organisations that engage dispute resolution service providers in a professional capacity. A client may not necessarily be a party to a dispute, but may engage a dispute resolution service provider to assist the resolution of a dispute between others.

D

Determinative dispute resolution processes are process in which a dispute resolution practitioner evaluates the dispute (which may include the hearing of formal evidence from the parties) and makes a determination. Examples of determinative dispute resolution processes are arbitration, expert determination and private judging.

Determinative case appraisal is a process in which the parties to a dispute present arguments and evidence to a neutral (the appraiser) who makes a determination as to the most effective means whereby the dispute may be resolved, without making any determination as to the facts of the dispute.

Dispute counselling is a process in which a dispute resolution practitioner (the dispute counsellor) investigates the dispute and provides the parties or a party to the dispute with advice on the issues which should be considered, possible and desirable outcomes and the means whereby these may be achieved.

Dispute resolution refers to all processes that are used to resolve disputes, whether within or outside court proceedings. Dispute resolution processes may be facilitative, advisory, evaluative, non-binding opinion or determinative. Dispute resolution processes other than judicial determination are often referred to as ADR.

Disputants. People/organisations in dispute, whether solely with each other or with additional parties, and whether already in litigation or not.

E

ENE (Early Neutral Evaluation) A preliminary assessment of facts, evidence or legal merits. It is a process in which the parties to a dispute present arguments and evidence to a qualified, trained neutral, at an early stage, for his or her non-binding opinion of the likely outcome. From this determination on the key issues in dispute the parties can then attempt to resolve the dispute by further negotiation.

Evaluative Mediation An approach to mediation where the parties can seek and obtain the non-binding advice of the mediator. He or she takes a relatively active or interventionist role, making suggestions or putting forward views about the merits of the case or particular issues between parties at their request. Using this process, parties may "test" the potential outcomes of a case. The mediator allows the parties to present their factual and legal arguments. He or she may then offer his or her own assessment or predictions as to a trial outcome. It is often used for more difficult cases, in which the gap between the parties is large, the issues are somewhat complex and the stakes are high.

Executive Tribunal A process, sometimes called 'Mini-Trial', in which parties make formal but abbreviated presentations of their best legal case to a panel of senior executives from each party, usually with a mediator or expert as neutral chairman. Following the presentations, the executives meet (with or without the mediator or expert) to negotiate a settlement on the basis of what they have heard.

Expert Determination A process in which an independent third party, acting as an expert rather than judge or arbitrator, is appointed by the parties to decide the dispute. There is no right of appeal, thereby giving parties finality.

F

Facilitative Mediation An approach to mediation where the neutral aids or assists the parties' own efforts to formulate a settlement. The mediator is in charge of the process but the parties are in charge of the content. This approach is sometimes referred to as 'interest-based' mediation. In this process, outcome control remains almost entirely in the hands of the parties and their representatives. A mediator enhances communication and helps to create options for resolution by ensuring that all relevant information is exchanged and heard by the parties. The mediator also helps to distinguish the parties' issues from their interests.

Face to Face (F2F) (Plenary/Joint Sessions) A meeting facilitated by a mediator which brings all those in dispute together to discuss issues and decide a way forward. This stage is not used during shuttle mediation.

Facilitative Dispute Resolution are processes in which a neutral assists the parties to a dispute to identify the disputed issues, develop options, consider alternatives and endeavour to reach an agreement about some issues or the whole dispute. Examples of facilitative processes are mediation, facilitation and facilitated negotiation.

Final Offer Arbitration ("baseball") – In this form of arbitration, which derives from the United States, the parties each separately submit a "final offer" to the arbitrator. The arbitrator chooses between the offer or the demand presented, based upon the arguments heard. It is called baseball arbitration because it was long used to resolve disputes between baseball players and teams.

H

Heads of Agreement The section of the settlement agreement in which the principal terms of the agreement are set forth.

I

Impartial A key principle that mediators must have no stake in the outcome of the process. Working without any investment in a solution.

Interventionist The degree of proactive involvement from a third party.

J

Joint Sessions (Plenary/Face to face) Stage in a mediation when the negotiating parties are brought together by the mediator. The Opening Joint Session takes the form of an introduction by the mediator and brief presentations by each party of their case at a round table meeting which may set the agenda and provide a vehicle for the controlled venting of emotional issues.

L

Litigation The process of bringing or contesting a law suit in which an impartial third party – the judge – receives evidence in support of the case and hears argument from each side after which a binding judgment is issued which can be enforced using the powers of the state. Litigation is an adversarial and usually public process that tends to create a winner and loser.

M

Med-Arb A process in which parties agree to mediate their dispute and, if unable to settle, they participate in binding arbitration using the same neutral. They contract to give the mediator power to 'convert' to being an arbitrator and make a legally binding award, in the event that mediated negotiations do not lead to a settlement.

Mediation A flexible process conducted confidentially in which an impartial, trained, mutually acceptable neutral third party helps two (or more) disputants work out how to resolve a conflict. The disputants, not the mediator, decide on the terms of any agreement reached. Mediation usually focuses on future rather than past behaviour, and is not concerned with blame or making findings of fact. Unlike judges or arbitrators, mediators have no authority to decide the dispute between the parties, although powerful mediators may bring to the table considerable capability to influence the outcome. Mediators may focus on facilitating communication and negotiation but they also may offer solutions and use leverage, including positive and negative incentives, to persuade the parties to achieve an agreement.

Mediation Agreement A document setting down the conditions under which the mediation will take place, including confidentiality, authority to settle, payment and role of the mediator.

Mediator An impartial, trained, mutually acceptable neutral person who helps disputing parties try to arrive at an agreed resolution of their dispute. Mediation cannot take place without a mediator, whose presence creates a new dynamic that is absent when parties undertake direct negotiation.

Multi-party Where a conflict or dispute involves more than two people, households, entities or organisations.

N

Negotiation A process in which disputants work out an agreement for themselves without the help of a third party, such as a mediator.

Neutral An individual who facilitates the ADR process, including mediators, arbitrators, adjudicators, private judges, facilitators, members of Dispute Boards and panellists.

Neutral Evaluation (see ENE) A process in which the parties to a dispute retain a neutral to provide a non-binding evaluation based solely on the merits of the case.

Neutral Expert Fact-Finding Used to help resolve a disputed technical issue, this may be a stand-alone, non-binding process or it can be part of a larger, non-binding process.

Non-Binding Arbitration A process that looks and feels like arbitration, but is advisory and non-binding.

O

ODR (On-line Dispute Resolution, eADR, cyber-ADR) are mediation services where a substantial part, or all, of the communication in the dispute resolution process takes place electronically, especially via online meeting platforms. This saves the parties and mediator from the cost of travel, cost of room hire and support, and is particularly useful where the participants are in different countries.

Opening Statements Oral presentations which are usually given in open plenary session after the Mediator's introductory address. These allow each party the chance to present an uninterrupted narrative of their case with the full force of feeling and certainty.

Ownership Ownership of an agreement is important in mediation, placing the emphasis on the fact that the parties themselves worked out a mutually satisfactory solution to their problem, and did not have it decided for or imposed upon them.

P

Parties are persons or bodies who are in a dispute that is handled through a dispute resolution process. In litigation the term is generally confined to people or entities in whom a cause of action is vested i.e. the claimant, and against whom the claim is brought, i.e. the defendant. In ADR the term is used in a wider sense to describe participants in the process.

Peer mediation Any use of mediation between peer groups, most usually when pupils and young people are trained to help others to try and resolve their disagreements. The term is also sometimes used to refer to mediators inside an organisation who mediate for their colleagues.

R

Reality Testing The method most commonly used by mediators to reduce party expectation. This tool involves attempting to get a party to understand the reality of his position by a self-evaluation of the strength of his case, his true BATNA, the costs consequences of the mediation failing, and the use of hypothesis in respect of outcomes. The use of the tool requires particular sensitivity, but can be vital for helping parties to adjust their position and become more flexible.

Reframing A tool used by mediators that involves changing party language by the use of more positive words, the complexion on words and circumstances and the order in which ideas are presented in order to allow a situation to be viewed more positively.

Reparation The act of making up for loss or injury. This may be financial, emotional or enacted through work. In Restorative Justice ADR processes, reparation is made either to the victim(s) of a crime, or to others within the community.

Respondent A person or organisation about whom a complaint is made.

Restorative Justice (RJ) A process in which mediative techniques are used to supports victims of crime, offenders and communities in seeking to repair the harm caused by crime, with mediation a favoured approach.

Round table meeting (RT) A meeting facilitated by a mediator or party representatives which brings all those in dispute together to discuss issues and decide a way forward. This stage is not used during shuttle mediation. In some disputes, for example personal injury claims or financial settlement of divorce, a round table meeting may precede mediation.

S

Settlement Agreement A brief document designed to set out in clear and understandable language the salient terms of a negotiated agreement. It has the effect in law of a contract, and therefore must be legal, sufficiently certain in its meaning, workable (i.e. the solution offered must be practicable) and enforceable.

Shuttle mediation A process in which the mediator/s talks separately to the parties, conveying their needs and suggestions to the others until a solution is found that is acceptable to all. This technique is also called caucusing, is sometimes used exclusively when the parties are reluctant to meet, although it may not be as effective in rebuilding relationships as joint meetings. The mediator may move between parties who are located in different rooms, or meet different parties at different times for all or part of the process.

T

Transformative mediation A model of mediation that focuses on the interaction between the parties, rather than resolution on favourable terms. The main function of the mediator is to provide an environment where empowerment and recognition between the parties can emerge and improve.

V

Victim-Offender mediation (see also **Restorative Justice**) is a process in which the parties to a dispute arising from the commission by one of a crime against the other come together with the assistance of a mediator.

W

Workplace mediation An informal way of resolving disputes at work which can be an alternative to formal grievance or disciplinary procedures, or employed before a case is referred to an employment tribunal to see if an agreed solution can be found. After cessation of employment the procedure is generally referred to as **Employment Mediation**.

2. EXAMPLES OF STANDARD FORM MEDIATION AGREEMENTS

i. Small Claims Track Agreement to Mediate

Name of Court	Claim No.
Name of Claimant	
Name of Defendant	

We, the parties, agree to enter into mediation of the above dispute, Claim No. ...., on the following terms and conditions:

1. The mediator

The parties agree to the appointment of *(insert name)*

as the court based mediator.

The parties understand that the mediator is independent, neutral, and is employed by Her Majesty's Courts Service (HMCS). The parties also understand that the role of the mediator is to facilitate settlement of the dispute by negotiation and agreement where it is possible. The mediator does not give legal advice and will not adjudicate the dispute.

The Mediator may ask the parties to consent to a co-mediator or observer to be present at the mediation if the parties agree. The parties may be asked to assist in the ongoing assessment of the present mediation scheme.

Save in the case of gross error or misconduct, the parties agree that they will respect the neutrality of the mediator, any professional body to which the mediator may belong, and HMCS, and not bring any claim, demands or proceedings against any or all of these, arising out of the appointment of the mediator or the conduct of the mediation.

2. Good faith and authorisation to negotiate

Whilst it is recognised that mediation is a voluntary process that enjoys the support of HMCS, and that the mediator will not, and cannot, compel the parties to settle, nor even to continue the mediation, the parties agree to participate in good faith with the aim of achieving settlement. The parties agree that they will have present at the mediation such people as are authorised to agree settlement terms, or ensure that they themselves have such authority.

3. Private sessions

During the mediation the mediator will probably speak to the parties separately in order to improve the mediator's understanding of the each party's views. Information given to the mediator during such private talks will be treated by the mediator as being confidential unless the party involved allows the mediator to give the information to the other party.

4. Confidentiality and the without prejudice nature of mediation

The parties agree to keep confidential the fact that mediation is to take place. Any information - whether written in a document prepared for mediation or written or spoken during the mediation - can only be used for the purpose of mediation and cannot be referred to in any court action unless the parties agree. The parties agree that they will not call the mediator to give evidence in any court action. The terms of the memorandum of agreement remain confidential, but if the memorandum of agreement forms part of a court order, the parties have permission to apply to the court for the purpose of enforcing those terms (if those terms are enforceable), or to claim for breach of the memorandum of agreement.

5. Ending the mediation

The mediator, or either of the parties, may end the mediation at any time without giving a reason. In that event the trial judge will only be aware that mediation has taken place and that it has failed.

6. Customer Feedback Questionnaire

HMCS would be very grateful if you could spend a few minutes completing our on-line survey so that we can learn from your experiences and ensure that our service is of the highest standard. You can access the survey at http://www.surveymonkey.com/s.aspx?sm=L2jj8Uo3DFunLrkKFZdbyQ_3d_3d

If you cannot access the internet, the mediator can provide you with a copy of the survey form.

Signed:

Claimant:	Defendant:
Mediator:	Date

ii. (Civil/Commercial) Mediation Agreement-to be signed by all involved in the mediation

This Agreement is made   2015 between:-

The First Participants c/o	**The First Participants' Solicitor** [ ] **of** [ ] **Solicitors** ("the First Participants' Representatives")
The Second Participants c/o	**The Second Participants' Solicitor of** (and any barrister, "the Second Participants' Representatives")
The Third Participants c/o	
Mediation Date and Time Booked	**2015 10.00 – 17.00**
Mediation Venue	[ ] Site Visit **[insert full address & postcode:** 10.00 Mediation Meeting **[TBC]**
Mediator	
Dispute	**[TBC] re**
Mediators Briefing Email	**2015**

IT IS AGREED by those signing this Agreement that:

1. The mediation services will be provided by the Mediator at the Mediation Venue in relation to the Dispute.

2. The Participants are taking part in this mediation in good faith with the aim of achieving common ground (and if time permits) a settlement of the Dispute. The Mediator's role is to help facilitate this. The First Participants and the Second Participants are authorised to agree terms of settlement and enter into a binding written settlement agreement if agreed and following legal or other advice (as they are recommended to do).

3. This mediation and all communications relating to it are without prejudice and are to be kept confidential by the Participants, the First Participants' Representatives and the Second Participants' Representatives, the Mediator and any observer. This includes all documents and correspondence produced for or at the mediation save where disclosure is required by law to implement or enforce the terms of any settlement agreement. The Participants may discuss the mediation with their professional advisers and/or insurers and will provide such information as they are obliged to do by law.

4. The Mediator shall not be liable to any Participant for any loss, damage or expense whatsoever arising in connection with this mediation. In the case of alleged negligence the Mediator's liability is limited to the amount of the professional indemnity insurance of which he has the benefit.

5. The Participants agree that they will not call the Mediator as a witness or expert nor require him to produce in evidence any records or notes relating to the mediation, in any litigation or other process. If any Participant makes any such application that Participant will indemnify the Mediator in respect of any costs relating thereto to include (but not limited to) reimbursement at the Mediator's standard hourly rate for any time spent resisting or responding to any such application.

6. No recordings or transcripts of the mediation will be made.

7. A settlement will only be legally binding if and when set out in writing and signed by or on behalf of the Participants.

8. The fees payable to the Mediator have been agreed per the Mediator's Briefing Email. The agreed fees will have been paid in cleared funds to the Mediators bank account (specified in the Invoice sent) before the Mediation Meeting. Any overtime, at the rate agreed per

the Mediator's Briefing Email. Each party will bear its own costs (if any) of participation in the mediation.

9. Form of Mediation

  9.1   Facilitative Mediation

    9.1.1 The Mediator will try to help resolve the Dispute by way of facilitative mediation, exploring issues, interests, needs and concerns of the Participants and assisting them independently and neutrally by generating options for a mutually agreed resolution of the matters in the Dispute. The Mediator Briefing Email explains what to expect at the mediation.

    9.1.2 Mediation is a voluntary process and the Mediator will not, and cannot, compel the Participants to settle. Either the Mediator or the Participants may terminate the process at any time.

  9.2   No Evaluative Mediation

    9.2.1 The Mediator does not offer evaluative mediation.

    9.2.2 The Mediator will not assess the merits of the Dispute or analyse or protect any Participant's legal position or rights.

    9.2.3 The Participants must (if they require an opinion on the merits of an issue, settlement, or proposal; or if they require legal advice) seek advice from their own chosen solicitor, or counsel.

10. Cancellations and Adjournments

  10.1 If the mediation is cancelled by any Participant more than 5 business days before the Mediation Date and is rescheduled, there is no cancellation fee for the first adjournment. Any time spent preparing for the Mediation Date will be noted and charged in the eventual billing. If more than one adjournment occurs, an adjournment fee of £250 may be charged at the discretion of the Mediator for each adjournment following the first payable before the Mediation Date.

10.2 If the mediation is cancelled within 5 business days before the Mediation Date and whether or not rescheduled, a cancellation fee of £400 plus preparation time notified (at £100 + vat per Participant) and any other incurred expenses is due and payable by the Solicitors for the Participants on or before the Mediation Date.

10.3 If the mediation is cancelled within 3 business days before the Mediation Date and whether or not rescheduled, a cancellation fee equal to the whole of the agreed mediation fee specified in the Mediator's Briefing Email including any other incurred expenses is due and payable on or before the Mediation Date.

10.4 Cancellations shall be in writing by the Solicitors for the Participants to the Mediator

11. This Agreement and the mediation is governed by the law of England and the Courts of England have exclusive jurisdiction to decide any matters arising out of or in connection with this Agreement or the mediation.

12. The referral of this dispute to mediation does not affect any rights under Article 6 of the European Convention of Human Rights, and if the dispute is not resolved through the mediation the Parties' right to a fair trial remains unaffected.

13. The Participants agree to an observer attending the mediation (usually a trainee mediator)

Signature of the First Participants: ....

Signature of the First Participants' Solicitor: ....

Signature of the Second Participants: ....

Signature of the Second Participants' Solicitor: ....

Signature of the Third Participants: ....

Signature of the Mediator: ....

Signature of the Observer:..

iii. Agreement to Mediate (Family Dispute)

AGREEMENT TO MEDIATE

Print name: **Signature:**   **Date:**

Print name: **Signature:**   **Date**

Please read the following and then sign

We have decided to use mediation to resolve issues between us and make our own plans for the future. Any proposals we reach may be written in a Memorandum of Understanding or Outcome Statement.

1. By signing this agreement, we express our sincere intention to attempt to:

   a) Be fair to each other throughout mediation

   b) Leave fault and blame out of the negotiations

   c) Be co-operative in resolving disagreements

   d) Consider - the needs of each child, our individual needs, each other's needs and the needs of the family as a whole

   e) Work for the least possible emotional and financial upheaval for all concerned

2. We understand that all communications, (except the disclosure of financial information) to which mediators are party, are made solely for the purpose of attempting to reach a settlement and are made on the basis that the communications are both (a) confidential and (b) will not be referred to in evidence in any court proceedings about the same issues. They will not be used in affidavits or statements.

3. Confidentiality

Mediation is a confidential process. Information will not be given, by the Service, to your legal or other advisers or to any other third party without first obtaining permission from both of you.

There are two exceptions to this confidentiality –

a) Risk of Harm

Where you or any other person (in particular a child) is, or is suspected to be, at risk of serious harm. In these exceptional circumstances we would normally discuss with each of you the action to be taken and where appropriate would contact the appropriate authority in line with the Family Mediator's Code of Practice.

b) Proceeds of Crime Act 2002

Certain disclosures in mediation may require us to make a disclosure to the appropriate government body under the Proceeds of Crime Act 2002 and/or the relevant money laundering regulations. We may also be under obligation, linked to this Act, to make such a disclosure without informing you that we are doing so. We have no choice in this matter where the Act or the regulations apply. We may also be required and/or choose to discontinue mediation.

4. We will only communicate with the mediators about issues in mediation during the sessions.

5. We agree to pay the Service according to the scale of charges

6. If one of us is unable to keep a scheduled appointment/s, he will notify the Service at least 1 working day in advance or as soon as possible in the case of a sudden illness. Less than 24 hours notice will incur a 50% fee charge.

7. We acknowledge that at no time will we receive financial, legal or other advice from the mediators or the service

8. We acknowledge that we have been told of the advantages of having separate solicitors to whom we will refer; before, during and at the end of mediation as appropriate.

9. Should a Memorandum of Understanding or Outcome Statement be prepared, we understand that it is not a legally binding document. However, we know that we can instruct a solicitor to prepare a legally binding document based on the Memorandum of Understanding or Outcome Statement.

10. If difficulties should arise in consultation with the solicitors, we will notify the mediator of the need for further discussions.

AIM and Finance & Property mediation only -

During the course of mediation we agree that:

a) We will make full, frank and true disclosures of finances and provide all supporting documentation.

b) We will not transfer, charge, conceal or otherwise dispose of any assets except for the purpose of providing for living necessities and expenses in the ordinary course of business

c) We will not make any further charges under any charge account for which both of us are legally responsible, unless mutually agreed upon

d) Financial disclosures are made on the basis that they are confidential to the Service but may be disclosed to our solicitors and may be used in evidence in Court

iv. Mediation/Arbitration Agreement for Property Redress Scheme (PRS) Disputes

PRS Ref:

This Agreement is made on [date] between:

Party A:
Party B:
(together referred to as "the Parties")
The Mediator:
And
Small Claims Mediation (UK) Ltd   (SCM)

in relation to a mediation ("the Mediation") to be held on

Date:	**TBC**
by:	**[telephone] [online]**
Time:	

IT IS AGREED by those signing this Agreement THAT:

The Mediation

The Parties agree to attempt in good faith to settle their dispute at the Mediation and to conduct the Mediation in accordance with this Agreement and consistent with the Small Claims Mediation Procedure and the Civil Mediation Council's Code of Conduct for Mediators current at the date of this Agreement (copies of which are available upon request from SCM).

The Mediation Process

The Mediation shall be conducted by telephone and/or electronic communication between the Parties and the Mediator on such basis as the Mediator shall deem to be most appropriate for the dispute. It will not normally involve the Parties in direct communication with each other.

The time allowed for the Mediation shall be a maximum of one hour commencing at a time agreed between SCM, the Parties, and the Mediator.

Arbitration (if not settled) *or Final Offer Arbitration (if not settled)*

The Parties further agree that, in the event that they are unable to reach a settlement during the time allocated for the Mediation, the Mediator shall immediately be, and is hereby appointed, as an Arbitrator in accordance with Section 16 of the Arbitration Act 1996. As an Arbitrator, the appointee shall consider the information provided to them during the course of the mediation proceedings, together with any other evidence requested by the Mediator that is submitted within the time period specified, and shall issue a binding and enforceable award in writing in accordance with Section 52 of the Arbitration Act 1996.

In the interest of arriving at a prompt and cost-efficient resolution of the dispute, the Parties hereby agree to dispense with the requirement for the Arbitrator to provide reasons for the Award, in accordance with Section 52 (4) of the Arbitration Act 1996.

Authority and status

The person signing this Agreement on behalf of each Party warrants that they have authority to bind that Party and all other persons representing that party at the Mediation to observe the terms of this Agreement, and that they also have authority to bind that Party to the terms of any settlement.

The Mediator, SCM and PRS shall not be liable to the Parties for any act or omission in relation to the Mediation or Arbitration unless the act or omission is proved to have been fraudulent or involved wilful misconduct, in which case liability shall lie with the person or organisation at fault.

Confidentiality and without prejudice status

Every person involved in the Mediation or Arbitration:

- agrees that all information passing between the Parties and the Mediator/Arbitrator, however communicated, is without prejudice to any Party's legal position and may not be produced as evidence or disclosed to any other decision-maker in any legal or other formal process, except where otherwise disclosable in law;

- agrees to their relevant personal data being used for the purposes of the Mediation or Arbitration;

- will keep confidential all information arising out of or in connection with the Mediation or Arbitration (save to the extent that it is already in the public domain);

- gives authority for the settlement agreement or Arbitration Award to be shared with SCM and PRS at the end of the Mediation or Arbitration;

- agrees that SCM or PRS may contact them after the Mediation or Arbitration to assess the level of satisfaction with the service;

- agrees that they and the others involved in the Mediation or Arbitration may disclose: the fact that the Mediation or Arbitration is to take place or has taken place; information where disclosure is required by law; information needed to implement or to enforce the terms of settlement or award; and may share with insurers, insurance brokers, accountants or solicitors such information as may reasonably be necessary to protect that person's legitimate interests.

Where a Party privately discloses to the Mediator any information in confidence before, during or after the Mediation, the Mediator will not disclose that information to any other Party or person without the consent of the Party disclosing it, unless required by law to make disclosure.

In any litigation or other formal process arising from or in connection with their dispute, the Parties will not:

- call the Mediator or any representative of SCM or PRS as a witness, expert, or consultant; or

- require the Mediator or any representative of SCM or PRS to produce in evidence any records or notes relating to the Mediation or Arbitration;

and if a Party makes an application in breach of this clause, that Party agrees to fully indemnify the Mediator, SCM and PRS in respect of any losses suffered or costs incurred (including the cost of time) in resisting and/or responding to such an application.

Settlement formalities

Settlement terms reached at the Mediation will be set out in writing by the Mediator and will be legally binding on the parties, even if they have not been signed or acknowledged by the parties in writing.

If the dispute has proceeded to Arbitration under the terms of this Agreement the Arbitrator shall issue a binding and enforceable Final Award to the parties in writing (including electronic communication), in accordance with Section 52 of the Arbitration Act 1996.

Legal status and effect of the Mediation

This Agreement is governed by the law of England and Wales and the courts of England and Wales shall have exclusive jurisdiction to decide any matters arising out of or in connection with this Agreement and the Mediation or Arbitration.

The referral of the dispute to the Mediation or Arbitration does not affect any rights that the Parties may have under Article 6 of the European Convention of Human Rights.

Signed:

Party A:

Party B:

3. SMALL CLAIMS MEDIATOR CODE OF CONDUCT

Introduction

11. This Code applies to any person who acts as a neutral third party ('the Mediator') in an ADR procedure under the auspices of Her Majesty's Courts Service.

Competence

12. The Mediator shall be competent and knowledgeable in the process of mediation. Relevant factors shall include proper training and continuous updating of their education and practice in mediation skills, having regard to any relevant standards or accreditation schemes.

Impartiality and conflict of interest

13. The Mediator will at all times act, and endeavour to be seen to act, fairly and with complete impartiality towards the Parties in the Mediation without any bias in favour of any Party or any discrimination against any Party.

14. Any matter of which the Mediator is aware, which could be regarded as involving a conflict of interest (whether apparent, potential or actual) in the Mediation, will be disclosed to the Parties. This disclosure will be made in writing to all the Parties as soon as the Mediator becomes aware of it, whether the matter occurs prior to or during the Mediation. In these circumstances the Mediator will not act (or continue to act) in the Mediation unless all the Parties specifically acknowledge the disclosure and agree, in writing, to the Mediator acting or continuing to act as Mediator.

15. Information of the type which the Mediator should disclose includes:

- having any financial or other interest (whether direct or indirect) in any of the Parties or in the subject matter or outcome of the Mediation; or

- having any confidential information about any of the Parties or in the subject matter of the Mediation.

Confidentiality

16. Subject to paragraph 8 below, the Mediator will keep confidential and not use for any collateral or ulterior purpose:

    - the fact that a mediation is to take place or has taken place; and

    - all information (whether given orally, in writing or otherwise) arising out of, or in connection with, the Mediation, including the fact of any settlement and its terms.

17. Subject to paragraph 8 below, if the Mediator is given information by any Party which is implicitly confidential, or is expressly stated to be confidential (and which is not already public), the Mediator shall maintain the confidentiality of that information from all other Parties, except to the extent that disclosure has been specifically authorised.

18. The duty of confidentiality in paragraphs 6 and 7 above will not apply if, and to the extent that:

    - all parties consent to disclosure;

    - the Mediator is required under the general law to make disclosure;

    - the Mediator reasonably considers that there is serious risk of significant harm to the life or safety of any person if the information in question is not disclosed; or

- the Mediator wishes to seek guidance in confidence from any senior officer of HMCS on any ethical or other serious question arising out of the Mediation.

Commitment and availability

19. Before accepting an appointment, the Mediator must be satisfied that he/she has time available to ensure that the Mediation can proceed in an expeditious manner.

Parties' agreement

20. The Mediator will act in accordance with the agreement (whether written or oral) made between the Parties in relation to the Mediation ('the Agreement to Mediate') (except where to do so would cause a breach of this Code) and will use his/her best endeavours to ensure that the Mediation proceeds in accordance with the terms of the Agreement to Mediate.

Withdrawal of Mediator

21. The Mediator will withdraw from the Mediation if he/she:

- is requested to do so by any of the Parties;

- is in breach of this Code; or

- is required by the Parties to do something which would be in material breach of this Code.

22. The Mediator may withdraw form the Mediation at his/her own discretion if:

- any of the Parties is acting in breach of the Agreement to Mediate;

- any of the Parties is, in the Mediator's opinion, acting in an unconscionable or criminal manner;

- the Mediator decides that continuing the mediation is unlikely to result in a settlement; or

- any of the Parties alleges that the Mediator is in material breach of this code.

4. EXAMPLE SETTLEMENT AGREEMENTS

7.12.1 Settlement Agreement

Name of court	
Claim No.	
Name of Claimant	
Name of Defendant	

On .... (date), the parties agreed that:

<u>Terms</u>

☐ The defendant will pay £ .... in full and final settlement no later than ...... (date) to claimant by cash/cheque/direct bank transfer.

☐ The action will be stayed and the parties will consent to an order in terms of the attached Tomlin Order.

☐ The action will be dismissed with no order as to costs.

☐ The agreement is in full and final settlement of any causes of action the parties to this dispute have against each other.

☐ This agreement supersedes all previous agreements between the parties.

☐ If any dispute arises out of this agreement, the parties will first attempt to settle it through the mediator before issuing enforcement proceedings through the court.

☐ The parties will keep the information contained in this agreement confidential and not use it for any collateral or ulterior purposes. Other than a final written agreement, any information - whether written in a document prepared for mediation or written or spoken during the mediation - can only be used for the purpose of mediation and cannot be referred to in any court action unless the parties agree. The parties agree that they will not call the mediator to give evidence in any court action.

Claimant:	Defendant:
Date:	Date:

5. Tomlin Order

Name of court	
Claim No.	
Name of Claimant	
Name of Defendant	

BY CONSENT IT IS ORDERED THAT

1. The claim is stayed on the terms of a confidential settlement agreement signed by the parties.

2. The parties have permission to apply to the court for the purpose of enforcing those terms (if those terms are enforceable), or to claim for breach of the settlement agreement. If no such application to restore is made by (insert date agreed by parties), the claim will stand dismissed.

If applicable

3. The hearing fixed for _____ is adjourned generally with liberty to restore / cancelled.

Claimant:	Defendant:
Date:	Date:

6. MEDIATOR CODES OF CONDUCT

EUROPEAN CODE OF CONDUCT FOR MEDIATORS

This code of conduct sets out a number of principles to which individual mediators may voluntarily decide to commit themselves, under their own responsibility. It may be used by mediators involved in all kinds of mediation in civil and commercial matters.

Organisations providing mediation services may also make such a commitment by asking mediators acting under the auspices of their organisation to respect the code of conduct. Organisations may make available information on the measures, such as training, evaluation and monitoring, they are taking to support the respect of the code by individual mediators.

For the purposes of the code of conduct, mediation means any structured process, however named or referred to, whereby two or more parties to a dispute attempt by themselves, on a voluntary basis, to reach an agreement on the settlement of their dispute with the assistance of a third person – hereinafter "the mediator".

Adherence to the code of conduct is without prejudice to national legislation or rules regulating individual professions.

Organisations providing mediation services may wish to develop more detailed codes adapted to their specific context or the types of mediation services they offer, as well as to specific areas such as family mediation or consumer mediation.

1. COMPETENCE, APPOINTMENT AND FEES OF MEDIATORS AND PROMOTION OF THEIR SERVICES

1.1. Competence

Mediators must be competent and knowledgeable in the process of mediation.

Relevant factors include proper training and continuous updating of their education and practice in mediation skills, having regard to any relevant standards or accreditation schemes.

1.2. Appointment

Mediators must confer with the parties regarding suitable dates on which the mediation may take place. Mediators must verify that they have the appropriate background and competence to conduct mediation in a given case before accepting the appointment. Upon request, they must disclose information concerning their background and experience to the parties.

1.3. Fees

Where not already provided, mediators must always supply the parties with complete information as to the mode of remuneration which they intend to apply. They must not agree to act in a mediation before the principles of their remuneration have been accepted by all parties concerned.

1.4. Promotion of mediators' services

Mediators may promote their practice provided that they do so in a professional, truthful and dignified way.

2. INDEPENDENCE AND IMPARTIALITY

2.1. Independence

If there are any circumstances that may, or may be seen to, affect a mediator's independence or give rise to a conflict of interests, the mediator must disclose those circumstances to the parties before acting or continuing to act.

Such circumstances include:

– any personal or business relationship with one or more of the parties;

– any financial or other interest, direct or indirect, in the outcome of the

mediation;

– the mediator, or a member of his firm, having acted in any capacity other than mediator for one or more of the parties.

In such cases the mediator may only agree to act or continue to act if he is certain of being able to carry out the mediation in full independence in order to ensure complete impartiality and the parties explicitly consent.

The duty to disclose is a continuing obligation throughout the process of mediation.

2.2. Impartiality

Mediators must at all times act, and endeavour to be seen to act, with impartiality towards the parties and be committed to serve all parties equally with respect to the process of mediation.

3. THE MEDIATION AGREEMENT, PROCESS AND SETTLEMENT

3.1. Procedure

The mediator must ensure that the parties to the mediation understand the characteristics of the mediation process and the role of the mediator and the parties in it.

The mediator must in particular ensure that prior to commencement of the mediation the parties have understood and expressly agreed the terms and conditions of the mediation agreement including any applicable provisions relating to obligations of confidentiality on the mediator and on the parties.

The mediation agreement may, upon request of the parties, be drawn up in writing.

The mediator must conduct the proceedings in an appropriate manner, taking into account the circumstances of the case, including possible imbalances of power and any wishes the parties may express, the rule of law and the need for a prompt settlement of the dispute. The parties may agree with the mediator on the manner in which the mediation is to be conducted, by reference to a set of rules or otherwise.

The mediator may hear the parties separately, if he deems it useful.

3.2. Fairness of the process

The mediator must ensure that all parties have adequate opportunities to be involved in the process.

The mediator must inform the parties, and may terminate the mediation, if:

– a settlement is being reached that for the mediator appears unenforceable or illegal, having regard to the circumstances of the case and the competence of the mediator for making such an assessment, or

– the mediator considers that continuing the mediation is unlikely to result in a settlement.

3.3. The end of the process

The mediator must take all appropriate measures to ensure that any agreement is reached by all parties through knowing and informed consent, and that all parties understand the terms of the agreement.

The parties may withdraw from the mediation at any time without giving any justification.

The mediator must, upon request of the parties and within the limits of his competence, inform the parties as to how they may formalise the agreement and the possibilities for making the agreement enforceable.

4. CONFIDENTIALITY

The mediator must keep confidential all information arising out of or in connection with the mediation, including the fact that the mediation is to take place or has taken place, unless compelled by law or grounds of public policy to disclose it. Any information disclosed in confidence to mediators by one of the parties must not be disclosed to the other parties without permission, unless compelled by law.

7. USEFUL CONTACTS

www.civilmediation.org; www.cmcregistered.org

The Civil Mediation Council is the recognised authority in the country for all matters related to civil, commercial, workplace and other non-family mediation. It holds a list of registered workplace mediation providers.

www.acas.org.uk

Acas is a public body responsible for improving organisations and working life through better employment relations. More information about what Acas can do to help is available on the Acas website,or from the Customer Service Team on 08457 38 37 36.

www.familymediationcouncil.org.uk

The Family Mediation Council (FMC) is made up of national family mediation organisations in England and Wales. Its website enables you to locate a family mediator.

www.mediationadvocates.org.uk

The Standing Conference of Mediation Advocates (SCMA) is a cross-professional organisation that provides a benchmark standard for those representing parties in mediation.

www.amati.org.uk

The Association of Mediation Assessors, Trainers and Instructors is a standards organisation which provides quality assurance for those seeking mediation training.

ABOUT THE AUTHOR

Andrew Goodman has been a barrister since 1978 and an accredited CEDR mediator since 1992 practising from chambers at 1 Chancery Lane, London in commercial, construction, partnership, franchising, professional negligence and farming disputes. He has been recommended as a leading junior in professional indemnity work and in ADR in the *Legal 500* for over 20 years. He is currently Professor of Conflict Management and Dispute Resolution Studies at Rushmore University, and is a sometime visiting lecturer on the LLM/LLB Dispute Resolution programme at University College, London, and the School of Oriental and African Studies. He is a trustee of the Centre for Peaceful Solutions, a north-London charity running family, community and restorative justice programmes. He holds an MBA in which he specialised in conflict management and a research PhD (Law) in mediation dynamics.

In November, 2007 Andrew helped launch the Standing Conference of Mediation Advocates of which he is Convenor. In that capacity he has since given training in mediation advocacy throughout the United Kingdom, and in Paris, Brussels, Berlin, Ankara, Lagos, Istanbul, Dubai, Muscat, Abu Dhabi, Kathmandu, Kuala Lumpur and Hong Kong. He has also advised members of the judiciary, ministries of justice and NGOs on the engagement of the legal profession with court-annexed mediation and top-down civil procedural codes in Belgium, Croatia, Nigeria, Ghana, Nepal, UAE and the People's Republic of China. He is on the Advisory Board of the Nepal International Arbitration Centre and the Editorial Board of its ADR Commercial Law Journal.

He was requested to submit evidence to Lord Woolf's Committee on Access to Justice on Court Annexed ADR Practices in other jurisdictions, and to Lord Justice Jackson's Review of Civil Costs. He is currently a member of the Bar's ADR Committee and a Bar Council mediation advocacy trainer, and a member of the Ministry of Justice Working Party on Business-Led Dispute Resolution and the Attorney-General's Pro-Bono Panel. He was Director of RICS Accredited Mediator Training 2007-2010 and remains deviser and course leader for the RICS APC course in Dispute Resolution and Conflict Management.

As Director of the Association of Mediation Assessors, Trainers and Instructors (AMATI), Andrew is regarded as one of the foremost international mediation trainers in the world. He is a member of the International Mediation Institute's Independent Standards Commission and Vic-Chair of its Mediation Advocacy Appraisal Sub-Committee.

Andrew is the author and editor of nearly 50 books including *Mediation Advocacy* (Mediation Publishing 2015, 3rd Edition), *Small Claims Procedure in the County Court – a Practical Guide to Mediation and Litigation* (Wildy, Hill & Simmonds 2010 5th2011 6th edn with HH Judge Pearl), *The Court Guide* (PPP Publishing 2011/12, 21st edn.) and *The Prison Guide* (Blackstone 1999). He wrote *The RCJ Guide* (Longman 1985) and *The Walking Guide to Lawyer's London* (OUP 2000), produced *The RCJ Plans* (Legastat 1988 onwards) and has had numerous articles published in the legal and academic press; he devised and edited *What's It Worth? Updated General Damages Awards in Non-Personal Injury Claims* (Vol. 1 Property Claims) (EMIS 2004). August, 2005 saw the publication of his seminal *How Judges Decide Cases: Reading, Writing and Analysing Judgments* (Xpl publishing), followed by its sequel *Influencing the Judicial Mind: Effective Written Advocacy in Practice* (Xpl 2006). In April 2006 he established Xpl-Professional Skills Training offering bespoke in-house specialist and advanced training in written advocacy and mediation representation/advocacy: see www.xpl-pst.com. He has written for *Commercial Lawyer* and appeared on Legal Network Television, Yorkshire Television, ITN News at Ten, the Discovery Channel, BBC Radio 4, Radio London, GLR and London Live, Radio Essex, Kent, Lancashire and the World Service. He has also written a number of books on late Victorian theatre and acted as a technical consultant on the Oscar-winning Mike Leigh film *Topsy-Turvy* and for a PBS documentary in the United States.

INDEX

Also Available

When Bank Systems Fail
Stephen Mason
Debit Cards, credit cards, ATMs, mobile and online banking:
your rights and what to do when things go wrong.
ISBN 978 185811 722 5

Email, Social Media and the Internet at Work
Stephen Mason
A concise guide to compliance with the law.
ISBN 978 185811 723 2

For these - and a wide variety of mediation titles - go to:

www.peerpractice.co.uk

9 781858 117140